Racial Spoils from Native Soils

Racial Spoils from Native Soils

How Neoliberalism Steals Indigenous Lands in Highland Peru

Arthur Scarritt

LEXINGTON BOOKS
Lanham • Boulder • New York • London

Published by Lexington Books
An imprint of The Rowman & Littlefield Publishing Group, Inc.
4501 Forbes Boulevard, Suite 200, Lanham, Maryland 20706
www.rowman.com

Unit A, Whitacre Mews, 26-34 Stannary Street, London SE11 4AB

British Library Cataloguing in Publication Information Available

Library of Congress Cataloging-in-Publication Data Available

ISBN 978-0-7391-9137-8 (cloth : alk. paper)
ISBN 978-0-7391-9138-5 (electronic)

∞ ™ The paper used in this publication meets the minimum requirements of American National Standard for Information Sciences Permanence of Paper for Printed Library Materials, ANSI/NISO Z39.48-1992.

Printed in the United States of America

To Margo, Luther, Fred, and especially Jill who has been there since the beginning.

Contents

Acknowledgments

In its long gestation, this book has amassed many debts. I first need to thank everyone in the village. I hope I was at least mildly entertaining and not too much of a burden. Special thanks go to the man I call Pedro here. Tercero and Consuela initially invited me to the village and generously hosted me, opening up not only their home but also the complex village history to me, thank you. I am much obliged to all the folks at CEDAP who provided such incredible openness and my initial connection to the village. Rómula Haritza and Max Carrasco in particular eased the daily toils of living. Thanks to Edilberto Jimenez Quispe who I thank in more detail in chapter 1. Jaymie Heilman and Caroline Yezer were fantastic roommates in Ayacucho, sharing peanut butter, debating perspectives, and otherwise dealing with the traumas of fieldwork. I blow you a wet *supi siki*.

Undertaking an ethnographic study through the Wisconsin Sociology Department proved a strange and perhaps unwise experience. I would not be the first or nearly the most prestigious person to say it is a place one has to survive rather than embrace. I had many good folks in my corner, though. Thanks go out especially to my advisor Gay Seidman and my committee Jane Collins, Karl Zimmerer, Jess Gilbert, and Phil Gorski. Is it odd to say that my dissertation defense was one of the best experiences I had in graduate school? My greatest resources were—and continue to be—my peers. Special thanks to Mark Harvey and Brad Manzolillo. When are we going to New Orleans again? Jeff Rickert: I will never forget those early years of struggle, and your shaking hand bombing the coffee all over the keyboard in our windowless computer lab. I am still mad at you for dying. Susie McDermott, née Mannon, you were incredibly generous with that big old brain of yours. Thanks for everything. Steve McKay, Molly Martin, Gary Chinn, Dimitri Kessler, Spencer Wood, Matt Vidal, and Cliff Westfall really helped make graduate school a good place. Brian Dill, thanks for the Wisconsin soiree. I feel lucky for our ongoing friendship. Diana Toledo and Scott Barnwell were amazing Madison friends—we will see you and the girls soon. Blake Gillespie and Joy Elizando should get a full paragraph at least—I will just say thanks here and fill in the details when I see you and your family next.

Since Wisconsin, I want especially to thank Eduardo Bonilla-Silva for encouraging me in my work. Thank you so much for reaching out. Tony Lucero and Maria Elena García have been unbelievably generous and positive. You have really helped me keep going. Thank you, too, David Stoll for your very positive words and critical readings of my works. And thank you for reviewing this book. Thanks to my editorial team at Lexington Books: Joseph Parry, Sarah Craig, Jana Hodges-Kluck, and Jay Song. Speaking of reviewers: I am glad for all the critical input from my anonymous reviewers throughout the years. You have made my work much stronger. But I have unfortunately experienced too much lack of professionalism with peer review as well. "Haters gonna hate," my students tell me. But editors at least should reject reviews that do not back up their condemning criticism. Yes, the work may be controversial. The litmus is whether it is original and well argued, not whether you agree with it.

I am so happy with my job at Boise State. I love my department and everyone in it. The students are incredible: open minded, passionate, smart, and dedicated. I only wish you were freer to pursue your educations. I have learned a lot from you. I hope this is mutual. In this, I would love to see the upper administration become more enlightened and beholden to the core concept of shared governance instead of seeing faculty as the problem and students as income. And speaking of imagining the impossible, I want to thank Slavoj Žižek whose works have taught me, among other things, of the tawdry cynicism that has bankrupted my generation.

And of course, my greatest thanks goes to my family. Thanks to James Scarritt for way more than I can even mention, but especially in this context for my entrée into the privileged world of academia and all the help with navigating its fierce, low-stakes battles. We've got to figure out the Scarritt and Scarritt publication. Thank you Prudence Scarritt for all you have done, particularly your steadfast critical and radical mind that I hope to do some justice to here. Thanks to Mimi and Eddye Lawley for making me part of your family and taking such good care of mine. As everyone knows, Jill Lawley has been and continues to be amazing. I am loving this journey with you. And I am lucky to be with you. Thank you, thank you, thank you. Margo, Luther, and Fred: I love hanging out with you and watching you grow. I do not want to miss any of your antics. You bring me nothing but joy. Thank you.

ONE

Introduction

How Does Racism Impoverish Indigenous People?

" . . . the farce is more fearful than the tragedy it follows."
—Herbert Marcuse, Epilogue to Marx's *Eighteenth Brumaire,* 1969

When Damian[1] mysteriously vanished from Huaytabamba, fellow villagers thought—even hoped—that someone had killed him. His swindles had robbed them of their wealth and left the village in shambles. Six years later, he returned unannounced and penniless. During his absence, residents had employed the unlikely means of converting to Evangelical religions to rebuild the trust and village institutions that Damian's machinations had shattered. And their new faith converted their wrath away from violent revenge and towards forgiving. Nevertheless, once home this same man again succeeded in cheating the villagers. Only this time it was for their lands, the core resource on which they depended for their existence.

This is not a story about hapless isolation or cruel individuals. Rather, this is a story about racism, about the normal operation of society that continuously results in indigenous peoples' impoverishment and dependency. This book explains how the institutions created for the purpose of exploiting Indians during colonialism have been continuously revitalized over the centuries despite innovative indigenous resistance and epochal changes, such as the end of the colonial era itself. The Huaytabamba case first shows how this institutional set up works through—rather than despite—the inflow of development moneys. It then details how the turn to advanced capitalism—neoliberalism—intensifies this racialized system, thereby enabling the seizure of native lands. Comparing these two instances reveals what is central to this form of domination. Contrasting

1

them addresses the changing nature of domination under global capitalism.

HUAYTABAMBA

"It is hard to believe we are so close to the city with all this poverty."
—NGO visitor to Huaytabamba

This statement typifies the reactions of the few urban visitors to Huaytabamba, surprised at impoverishment despite such geographic proximity
to the urban core. Other studies in the Andes share such sentiments,
looking at remote locales and concluding that such conditions result from
neglect and abandonment.[2] The poor Peruvian infrastructure hobbles the
wellbeing of the many far-flung villages. And, indeed, the ideology of
social neglect pervades the villages themselves—mixed in a rich cocktail
of distrust, resentment, and fatigue with all things urban. While remote-
ness and poverty do correlate, they fit only weakly with the record of
colonialism. Thus, in looking at the highly proximate village of Huaytabamba, I investigate how poverty persists because of—not despite—its
articulation with the city. In this way I can speak beyond the experiences
of a single village to the complex social web of institutions and cultural
practices—of which the village is but a single organization—that heavily
bind community and villager experiences.

While I initially came to Huaytabamba to look at other issues, the
domination of local life by a small group of men quickly became the most
pressing concern. Adding complexity, villagers regularly denounced
these men for malfeasance, yet continued to entrust them with policy
decisions, labor, and money. Explaining their power became the obvious
focus of my work. Where does it come from? How is it so extreme? Why
did villagers continually support them despite open acts of corruption?
And, perhaps most importantly, how does it speak to the integration of
indigenous populations into national and global society?

Huaytabamba is a one-hour, twelve-kilometer bus ride from the city
of Ayacucho. The main, paved highway to the coast makes up half of the
route, while poorly maintained narrow dirt roads more typical of the
contemporary Andes cover the rest. Though villagers had built a road all
the way to the community, cars almost never visited. Yet villagers regularly made the trip to the city, as it was the hub of socioeconomic activities. Villagers therefore did not overly suffer from geographic isolation;
but the ability to visit the city did not readily translate into access to its
institutions.

At 9,000 feet above sea level, the city of Ayacucho itself is literally the
end of the paved road, boasting a population of 100,000. The macadam
ribbons its way from the coast, over the Andes and back down to Ayacucho, a bus trip of over eight hours. The central highway passes through

Ayacucho from Huancayo in the north on its way to Cuzco to the south. This gravel highway narrows to one lane in places and is frequently washed out in the rainy season. The climate is arid and moderate except when the rainy season brings torrential downpours flooding the city.

The economy is almost exclusively agricultural. Huanta just to the north, lower in elevation and hotter in temperature, is a major production area, particularly for tropical and semi-tropical fruit. But the most lucrative connection runs over a 15,000-foot pass and down the Andes to the east to the lush coca-growing areas at the edge of the Amazon basin, what they call the *ceja de la selva*, the eyebrow of the jungle. A variety of small towns and villages spread in all directions from Ayacucho. Higher elevation locales can easily get frost and focus more on cattle and Andean tubers while more fertile inner montane valleys grow a variety of fruits and vegetables.

The city is known for its high amount of Catholic churches, one for every year of Christ's life though many residents say this lavish outlay was required to quell the rebellious indigenous groups of the area. Elaborate Carnival and Holy Week celebrations give the normally sleepy city a lively party atmosphere. As the departmental capital of one of the poorest regions, Ayacucho holds the dubious honor of birthing the extremist Maoist guerrilla group Sendero Luminoso—and being a primary victim of the army's ruthless counterinsurgency campaign. Now a battle rages between nongovernmental organizations (NGOs) who struggle to access international funding, especially as the government has dramatically reduced social spending. Indeed, city workers covet NGO positions more than any other, both in terms of prestige and income.

The road westward climbs to Huaytabamba after passing through its small provincial capital. This sports a large cement main square surrounded by a grid of gravel streets for three blocks in all directions. The small bus or *combi* trudges up beyond the provincial seat, passing the turn off for two villages until it stops on a ridge. Huaytabamba villagers have to walk uphill from this point, following the road until a footpath cuts up a small drainage to more directly reach the village. The community itself has two parts separated by this drainage. The upper section hosts the central square, communal house, elementary school, and most of the houses. The village sits at 12,000 feet in a crescent shaped bowl of patchwork hills climbing to over 14,000 feet.

Villagers primarily speak Quechua, the indigenous language spread by the Incan Empire. No electrical services come to the village, though a power line passes directly through. Villagers live in small compounds of three or four squat adobe buildings. Each has a living quarters, a kitchen, and then dedicated farming buildings for storing potatoes, grains, and tools. Cooking takes place over an open fire of eucalyptus, filling the small kitchens with eye burning smoke. The women cook and then clean the dishes in small plastic basins. I ate with a family once whose little lamb "Bebito," that the children carried around like a doll, trod all over the clean dishes after a meal much to everyone's amusement.

The drinking water system, installed through a grant from the Ayacucho hospital but using villager labor, runs pipes down from the high pastures. While passing through purification tanks, the system is actually creatively patched together. Villagers creatively use any material to insure water flow—though what is delivered desperately needs boiling to purify. Most people have spigots at or near their houses. People have access to outhouses. And, together, the water and latrines mean that the village meets the minimum standards for elevation above dire poverty.

IN THE VILLAGE

The average villager holds three acres of lands in diversified plots, though there is a range from the landless to over ten acres. Only about ten percent of the land, in the lowest corner of the village, has irrigation. The remainder relies on rain so it sits idle in the dry season. A large stand of eucalyptus crowns the hill immediately above the village. Pastures spread beyond that, with only a few high fields employed for hearty tubers. Villagers practice several forms of mutual labor exchange, predominantly the *faena*, in which all families work on village projects (such as cleaning irrigation canals), and the *ayni*, where some mutuality (including limited paid labor) regulates groups working in fields controlled by individuals.

The comunidad generally governed itself, periodically electing a presidential junta, though was also connected to a district mayor and district governor. Villagers served as representatives of each system. And no external funding came to any of the bureaucracies. The comunidad guarantees access to land, safeguarding against taxation and expropriation through requiring participation in labor parties and regular meetings—or compensating in cash or kind. Until the 1960s, a hacienda occupied this spot. Four main families—workers on the hacienda—established the village by gathering sufficient people together to purchase the land from the hacienda. The patriarchs of those families are known collectively as the *cabecilla*, a title that comes with high local influence although all four cabecilla members are illiterate. The terrible violence of the 1980s civil war touched but did not radically alter the village, pushing many villagers to spend more time in the city and commute to their lands.

The median villager income floated below US$300 a year, well less than the requirements for caloric reproduction. But this is not a fully cash economy. Barter existed with villages in different production zones. And villagers paid no taxes so incurred no running costs on their houses and lands. Wages and market sales were more about accessing cash for purchases. Villagers needed money for basics like clothing and school supplies. But they also bought a host of farming inputs such as fertilizer, pesticide, and tools. There were also many sociocultural practices requiring money, such as festivals, soccer tournaments, and weddings.

Accessing cash was one of the major struggles for villagers. While dedicating much of their harvests to self-reproduction, they also sold to wholesalers in Ayacucho. They marketed some of their livestock, though these served more as a form of long-term savings. Income mostly came through wage work. Sometimes aynis paid in cash or kind, so people did not have to leave the village. But people generally had to travel to work. Short term, people bussed to Ayacucho to seek manual labor. This paid the minimum wage of US$3.50 per day, with transport to and from the village sucking up twenty percent of this. Especially in the dry season, people migrated to other areas for paid wages, such as the jungle areas or where there were ongoing large infrastructure projects. Families sent members to different places to diversify their income streams and mitigate risk although migration incurred risks and costs of its own.

I lived in both the village and the city of Ayacucho, as did several of the residents themselves. In the village, I stayed in a small extra room belonging to one family with which I shared many meals. My lack of working Quechua made immediate, intimate communication difficult. But my alien presence created just as many difficulties, both in learning what was going on in the village and by increasing the hardships involved with conducting my work and generally getting by day to day. I was happy I could curl up into my sleeping bag when the sun went down at six and not wake until it returned in twelve hours. As the weeks wore on, I continued living and working in the fields alongside villagers. With this stability, my position became less of a curiosity, with villagers calling me a *yerno* (son-in-law) of the community, but still regarding me somewhat as a mascot they could be proud of.

While I always felt a deep sense of alienation, my relationship with villagers changed dramatically once I became directly embroiled with Damian's struggle to privatize everyone's fields. I cannot overemphasize how successful this interventionist or activist method proved in terms of quality and quantity of information (Hale 2008). Leaders on both sides of this polarized debate began seeking me out and explaining their actions and perspectives. Almost all of the other villagers similarly desired or were willing to discuss this major issue with me and to tie it to other events in the community's history. While some of the more astute players, Damian in particular, plied me with an overabundance of information, they strategically kept things from me. But Huaytabamba is a small village, with all residents sharing some form of kin relation. Secrets did not stay secret long. While my role in these events proved of little significance, the sheer quantity of information made triangulation remarkably straightforward. This not only allowed me to tell a coherent story, it enabled me to read deeply into my various sources, such as actions by urban personnel, interviews, and the community minutes largely written by the elite sons of the village.

Overall, my strangeness, persistence, and interference helped me gain a relationship with villagers sufficient to dialogue with them about their lives. But, really, it was the continued generosity and humor of villagers that enabled whatever achievement I have gained. To my knowledge, I acquired several nicknames. The most persistent one was *pala chaki*, a Quechua-Spanish amalgam meaning shovel foot, a nice reference to my relatively towering size. I hope this at least testifies to villagers humorously enduring my presence. Though I was in pretty good physical shape when conducting my research, my hands blistered under the toils of farming. And when otherwise "reciprocating" with my free labor, people could not help but make comments such as: "so large but so little strength." Hopefully, though, the strength of my training will shed light into Huaytabamba's place in the larger world.

NEOLIBERALIZING THROUGH RACE

The global capitalist system has always had populations superfluous to its functioning, but neoliberal reforms have dramatically increased these numbers. William I. Robinson (2004) estimates these as up to half of the people in some third world countries, and up to a third of the global population. These populations have been reduced to what social scientists term bare life conditions. In cases like those of native peoples, capitalist interests "covet the dowry, but not the bride" as Israeli Prime Minister Levi Eshkol said of the Palestinians. Lands no longer serve as holding grounds for relative surplus labor, but as potential areas of resource extraction in which the population is only worthy of removal. Further, these outcomes prove highly racialized, with the mechanisms of expulsion disproportionately targeting darker complected peoples (Robinson 2013).

At the same time, the financial capital that dominates global exchanges exerts an ever-increasing demand for public resources to convert into private profits. Before financial deregulation, capitalism made profits through the production process adding value to the sum of the overall inputs. Manufacturing therein generated an unprecedented abundance. In contrast, financial capitalism centers on rent collection. Rather than paying for the value added through production, profit comes from making people pay to access things that have become privately owned and operated. Advanced capitalism has therefore innovated a wide range of mechanisms to expropriate all manner of goods into its circuits. This includes services like education and health care, but also converts a variety of former rights and regulations into moneymaking ventures, such as windfalls from currency speculation. With the financialization of the economy, previously protected areas have become increasingly subject to raw material extraction, generating booms in countries like Peru. Opening resources to privatization and speculation creates spectacular though short-lived growth—bubbles. But overall economic growth stagnates. David Harvey (2005) terms this *accumulation by dispossession* because it is about taking rather than making things.

Advanced capitalism therein invigorates the age-old practice of land expropriation through providing titles. Regularizing documentation may seem like a process of protecting landholdings. But titling amounts to powerful interests imposing a new system onto an old. Though there are some exceptions, this makes titling the archetype of primitive accumulation, of taking rather than making. In England, as Karl Marx (1867) famously recounts, centuries of such processes, written only "in letters of blood and fire," robbed people of their land, eventually generating enough funds to underwrite capital-intensive industrialization while supplying factories with powerless workers. In the United States after the Mexican-American War, the government imposed private titles on Spanish and Mexican communal land grants, initiating a rapid process of land loss. And Tania Murray Li (2010) describes a huge variety of such processes stretching from colonialism to the present day. This dynamic, now expanded into a wide range of goods and services beyond land, allows capital access to cheaper inputs for increasing profitability and lowering risks (Harvey 2003, 139).

The rentier economy also enables an unprecedented concentration of wealth and power. Elites can easily capture and hoard the windfall profits now not attached to the costs of production. Further, rentiers have incurred no obligation to redistribute wealth to the general population. With production deemphasized, compliant middle and working classes become peripheral. The elites of financial capital therein do not face the old issues of how to reliably exploit populations. Instead they confront issues of how to control them. The managers of global capitalism therein face a double-sided question: (1) how to make more resources renderable to the needs of financial capital, and (2) how to control the growing population of the dispossessed.

Especially as manifest in highland Peru, this book argues that this neoliberal question is actually a colonial question, in fact, *the* Colonial Question, also termed the Indian/Native Question/Problem: how does a small foreign minority dominate a much larger and potentially hostile indigenous majority? Much more forcefully than previous works, this book argues that the answer is race, particularly the way it has been historically institutionalized, practiced, and contested. In other words, rather than this being a neoliberal process with racial outcomes, this is a process of colonial racial domination vitalized through neoliberal reforms. As such, this book can help more deeply theorize the racial role in neoliberalism, particularly how this colonial legacy enables the rapid and broad spread of the class project for the restoration of elite power.

The beginning insight for my argument is that the neoliberal challenge has long been the primary ruling conundrum of elites in peripheral capitalist countries like Peru. Lacking any real industrial base, such elites depend for their economic wellbeing and their means of social control on selling natural resources on the global market, a traditional form of rent collecting. Instead of raising standards of living, elites use the profits gained under the rationale of comparative advantage to police the populace, preserving their ability to collect rents and their monopoly on power. Extraction generates popular alienation that needs policing. But extraction inherently involves ever-increasing costs of production as the goods do not become replenished but rarer with each shovel full. The volatility of the global markets in raw materials exacerbates this precariousness. Maintaining any kind of consistent income, let alone increases, presses elites to ever expand the territory dedicated to extraction and thus their policing activities. Hence the traditional ruling conundrum of peripheral capitalism: how to simultaneously increase resource extraction (rents) and control over the increasingly alienated population. Elites have most robustly answered this colonial question through creating and exploiting stark racial divides.

PERU: AUTHORITARIANISM AND RACIAL SPLINTERING

"Peru, today and in the past, is best characterized by the presence of islands of governmentality in a sea of sovereignty." (Drinot 2011, 186)

Over twenty years of intellectual common sense insists on the inherent unity of native communities and the irrelevance of race in their social dynamics. At its best, the unity claim asserts patrimonial rights about indigenous self-determination, offering protections to some of the most vulnerable populations. But this holds the people who have experienced some of the worst traumas up to the highest expectations, with the corollary that a lack of unity forfeits native rights, a racial trope that too frequently has disempowered indigenous interests. Further, in obscuring local divisions this idea can enable the most ruthless and exploitative to speak on behalf of natives. At their best, the anti-race claims attempt to counter essentialist thinking about the inherent inferiority of natives. This denial, however, sweeps up the social category of race, negating the real group experiences of oppression and the cumulative socioeconomic outcomes of existing systems of subordination. Race truly has no biological basis. But denying its social reality is a classic color-blind racist trope that leaves a whole host of deleterious outcomes only explained by the failings of individuals, further disempowering the racially marginalized.

Against this grain, Rudi Colloredo-Mansfield (2009, 13) finds that "old racial markers did not so much disappear as metastasize . . . have become acknowledged internal differences of native communities." Indigenous spaces are riven by difference and conflict. In the epigraph above, Paulo Drinot says that the islands of urban inclusive citizenship are surrounded by an authoritarian-run sea of the rural. In his larger argument, Drinot moves beyond the limits of his metaphor to argue that the capitalist project of the central state relies on fostering a racist "essentialist fear" of native populations. This marks natives as hostiles in need of being controlled rather than governed, and without legitimate claim to the various natural resources over which they inconveniently reside.

While showing the local importance of race, Colloredo-Mansfield also indicates that the village is not the primary race-making institution even as these dynamics get played out here. What then are the institutions that make race matter and how are they related to the village? Drinot shows the state as a primary race-making institution and its ideological role in perpetuating authoritarian rule. "García's capitalist revolution," he finds, "ultimately, is an attempt to overcome indigeneity, to de-Indianize Peru," and as such is a highly racist attack on natives, justifying the continuance of disciplinary rule (Drinot 2011, 183). This model represents an intensification of state mestizaje, or the assimilation of Indians into the improved mestizo race—or their destruction if unwilling or unable. He therein further stresses the colonial aspect of such rule. In this, however, he insinuates but in no way specifies the means through which sovereign rule is actually exercised. He establishes solidly that urban mestizo reality depends on authoritarian rule of the native countryside and that the state empowers it. But he leaves unspecified the actual processes through which native subordination is achieved.

Putting these analyses together insinuates a relationship between rural authoritarianism and racial fracturing. Colloredo-Mansfield rhetorically asks as a major driving question of the age: "do indigenous communities really challenge racism or replicate it, hoarding opportunities among prosperous sectors and isolating poorer ones?" To this Drinot's analysis adds: how does the situating of villages within the larger relations of rule work to reproduce or challenge the racist projects of the central state? In sum, these two quotes stress (1) the relegation of native spaces to authoritarian forms of control and (2) the racially splintered nature of local reality. But they leave the connections between these unaddressed. This book looks to specify these connections, highlighting crucial processes through which localized racial splintering brings about central state priorities for controlling indigenous populations through excluding them.

INSTITUTIONALIZED RACISM

One route for inquiring into these issues that is highly underdeveloped in the Latin American context entails investigating the racialized social structure: how society is organized so as to perpetuate racial disparities. Critical race theory emphasizes that racial inequality is not so much the result of disparaging attitudes or the holdover from historical events, but an evolving political system grounded in the initial European colonial project (Omi and Winant 1994; Goldberg 2002; 2009; Ansell 2006). Conquest and colonization created the current concept of race and reshaped the world around it, operating through a "logic of circular and cumulative causation," in which inequalities build further inequalities to create a durable system (Tilly 1998; Winant 2001). As such, race became a central defining aspect of modernity: global capitalism was built on trafficking African slaves; the nation-state depended on an uncivilized dark other for its coherence; and Enlightenment ideas championed and even scientifically proved wealthy European males inherently superior to all others (Winant 2001). This established a global system of European male privilege predicated upon the subordination of darker peoples, leading to the naturalization of a de facto "two-tiered, morally partitioned population divided between white persons and nonwhite subpersons" (Mills 1998, 108).

These works emphasize that, once racialized, the normal organization and practices of society perpetuate racial subordination, engendering racial contestation while simultaneously rendering it largely invisible (Bonilla-Silva 1997). Rather than a discrete variable, race permeates all aspects of society so that the "mundane features of the social world that at first sight do not appear to be racialized but, when analysed within an inductive, theoretical framework, are found to be directly and indirectly relevant to the construction of race as a social phenomenon" (Holdaway 1997, 396). *Racism*, rather than an aberration or an individual psychological disturbance, largely entails perpetuating the system of inequality. The system ensnares the individuals it produces into perpetuating racial inequality through their everyday actions. While troubling for well-meaning whites, this dynamic creates serious dilemmas for minorities who, in some way or another, must participate in their own subordination (Collins 1996). Overall, then, understanding durable racial inequalities requires investigating how the interacting structures and everyday practices of society generate a historically emergent racialized social structure (Bonilla-Silva 2001, 48).

INDIRECT RULE AND NATIVE RACIAL SUBORDINATION

So what does the Peruvian racialized social system consist of and how does it subordinate native peoples? In exploring this question, my work continues the tradition of investigating the Indian Question or Native Problem, namely: how does a small minority of European descent dominate a larger and potentially hostile indigenous population? Throughout Peruvian history, dominant groups have most robustly answered this question with indirect rule. Indirect rule provides a deeper key to understanding indigenous subordination in that it elucidates a historically emergent structure through which localized authoritarian power is linked to urban citizenship regimes. In other words, this provides a means for understanding the articulation between Drinot's islands and sea: how the self-government by free mestizo people in the city depends upon the arbitrary despotic rule over native people in the countryside. In this, indirect rule must be seen as the preeminent state form linking Foucault's (2000) governmental and sovereign power, as the most efficient and effective way for a small minority to dominate a much larger majority regardless of the trappings of any explicit colonial leadership.

This system racially subordinates natives through dividing them ethnically. This amounts to an institutional segregation of two distinct but hierarchical governing frameworks. While most obviously manifest in the geographic divide between the native countryside and the European town, it is the bifurcation of the state that causes this physical separation. Urban institutions operate through modern inclusionary forms of civil government, but with this civilization predicated upon the disenfranchisement of the Indian Other. Rural governance, in contrast, consists of the (central authority defined) traditional practices of vesting all legislative, administrative, executive, and judiciary power in single individuals.

Since its establishment at conquest, dominant groups have regularly revitalized this system, providing it with new resources to adapt it to changing circumstances and the diverse challenges pushed by native peoples (see chapter 2). Overall, the governance of native peoples amounts to a system of decentralized despotism (cf. Mamdani 1996). Dominant groups rule over native areas "on the cheap" by creating authoritarian local positions granted *carte blanche* to provide rural quiescence. Natives in turn must depend upon these intermediaries for their personhood. The system generates its own resistance, though this tends to be focused on the local despots, therein exacerbating the ethnic splintering that undergirds racial domination. In all, the preservation of local authoritarian positions dependent upon native fragmentation, and upon whom natives depend for access to the urban core, ensures that the goals of the central state are achieved: a fractured and compliant peasantry.

Ethnicity, though, plays a much more complex and contestatory role, even as the bifurcated state skews it in favor of its fracturing function.

Ethnicity, with all apologies to Stewart Hall, is the modality in which race is lived. In terms of sociocultural practices aimed at group betterment, ethnicity in highland Peru assumes two forms: one of group mutuality and another of allegiance to the locally powerful. Local groups attempt to improve themselves either through enabling horizontal connections facilitating working together for mutual interests, or through capitalizing on the privileges of the elite by concentrating power in their hands. These are qualitatively different but they are not mutually exclusive. In fact, local social stability generally requires the obscuring of their distinction.

Group mutuality lies at the core of ethnicity in general and in the Andes specifically. But such coordinated efforts work better with greater resources (see Lucero 2008). This makes more privileged members more valuable and the mutuality asymmetrical. Elites can therein draw on local strictures against shirking in order to make people participate in the ethnic projects they initiate, and potentially increase their power. At some point the asymmetry can shift to predominate so that group wellbeing depends mostly on elite wellbeing—meaning that the system turns largely exploitative. The opacity between these forms means that (1) the extent of both exploitation and group betterment can largely only be seen retrospectively, and (2) the system is highly enabling of exploitative activities by the elite—group mutuality is variously a tool of elite exploitation. The larger racialized state structure further biases these relations to favor the elite-centered version, making ethnicity a primary tool of domination and exploitation.

The ethnic character of racial domination does not generally mean that ethnicity spans different races, but rather speaks to the hybrid character of elite figures whose emphasized racial status shifts according to their institutional setting. These are contingent and contested grounds. But they are the primary terrain through which local politics occur. Further, the contours and content enabling racialized indirect rule have made important changes across history.

ANDEAN RACISM THROUGH TIME

As I explore in chapter 2, the Peruvian system has endured despite creative indigenous resistance and epochal transformations such as Independence and neoliberalism. Spanish colonialism racialized the natives in order to exploit them, classifying them ideologically and institutionally as inherently inferior beings. This ushered in draconian policies that decimated the population through degrading living and working conditions and cycles of genocidal violence (Wolf 1982; Klarén 2000; Postero 2007). But a simultaneous re-ethnicization splintered regional populations into highly localized identities based on the European-backed authorities who provided the only, albeit highly paternalistic, protection in this exploitative system. These local state proxies have had various names throughout history, including *cacique, gamonal, caudillo, tinterio,* and *hacendado.*

Patronage has long fueled this Peruvian variety of racialized rule. The Crown had to control a huge new territory and population dwarfing its home domain. Racialized patronage enabled it to do so. Spanish settlers enjoyed the unique rights granted only to the civilized people of Europe, as established in the *Régimen de Castas* and other laws enforcing the racial hierarchy (Morner 1966). Lavishing rewards upon these citizens, including land tracts larger than many current U.S. states, ensured a continual flow of goods and labor from the primitives in need of Enlightened European guidance (Klarén 2000). As their sole link to the outside world, native wellbeing depended upon the success and beneficence of their local patron. The system thereby forced natives to provide tributes to the extremely powerful local individual whose own position depended upon continuing native fragmentation. Moreover, this extreme form of paternalism heavily enforced the racial hierarchy by forcing the native subpersons to depend almost exclusively on their local European citizen without the possibility of ever achieving this personhood themselves (cf. Mills 1998).

The preeminence of paternalist exchanges has thereby long enabled racialized governance. This system dominates through providing rather than denying resources. And it does so in order to enable an efficient if cruel means of control—rather than other ostensible goals such as saving souls, personal fulfillment, or raising standards of living. Further, the state structure made paternalist racialization the easiest path to follow—any deviation requiring tremendous effort—ensuring the continuation of racial inequality.

State policies have reproduced this racialized authoritarian model as an explicit part of the major transitions since colonialism—independence, nation-state formation, land reform, developmentalism, and globalization (cf. Mallon 1995; Thurner 1997). As Pierre L. van den Berghe and George Primov (1977) found for rural areas in the 1970s:

> The mechanisms for maintaining inequality are so solidly entrenched and so thoroughly routinized that unequal relations take place under a veneer of benevolent despotism on the part of the dominant group and ingratiating subservience on the part of the dominated group. (127–30)

While these historic disruptions presented major opportunities to shift to more inclusive models, the regular outcomes retrenched decentralized despotism through providing it with new resources and innovations. Further, as the above quote indicates, these exploitative relations have become thoroughly naturalized, understood as a normal aspect of daily relations and therefore not fully necessitating coercive enforcement.

Three important and intertwining changes altered this system during the last half of the twentieth century without changing its overall authori-

tarian form. Throughout Latin America, governments and societies variously turned from ideas of inherent racial superiority towards an all-
inclusive model of the mestizo Cosmic Race—a *sui generis* people emerging from the union of natives and Europeans (Vasconcelos [1925] 1979).
Mestizaje (becoming mestizo) newly promised universal citizenship
through a celebration of the native heritages of the Americas—though
only as a mix with European stock. As it strove for inclusivity, then, state
mestizaje simultaneously renovated racism, delivering "a double blow,
denigrating the unassimilated while inciting the assimilated to wage an
endless struggle against the 'Indian within'" (Hale 2004, 17). Citizenship
became more inclusive, but only through creating a new sector whose
rights depended upon continually proving their deservingness by denigrating natives.

Soon after mid-century, mestizaje became interwoven with the emerging developmentalist ideas of progress through industrialization spear-
headed by an interventionist state (Drinot 2011). The governments not
only promoted a specific capitalist agenda, they tied it to novel assimilationist policies. This was evidenced most obviously when states, responding to rural discontent, turned natives into peasants with a quick
slash of their pens. While promising greater enfranchisement, these reforms traded native patrimonial rights for the class rights to work the
soil, effectively divorcing any local victories from demands for larger
changes to the system of racialized rule. At the same time, state mestizaje
created a new middle stratum that personified the developmentalist
progress that promised to transcend the old governing ideas of racial
degeneration. This group carried a powerful authority regarding modern
progress. Developing meant becoming mestizo. Thus the contrast with
indigenous peoples only became sharper, natives now denigrated as anti-
modern barriers to economic advancement. Specific policies institutionalized this, such as cheap food making the growing urban mestizo working
class depend on the stagnation of rural indigenous agricultural production. Chapter 3 details the key racialized processes through which the
rural links to the urban core exclude indigenous people through mestizo
developmentalist inclusion.

By the end of the twentieth century, rapid policy changes beginning
with President Fujimori's authorship of a new constitution in 1992,
ushered in a transition from developmentalism to neoliberalism, significantly altering the terms and resources for decentralized despotism.
Worldwide neoliberal reforms simultaneously generated massive inequalities, extractive commodity booms, and a dramatic increase in populations superfluous to capitalist production. Under these conditions, the
controlling function of Peruvian indirect rule became ever more important (chapter 5). But these reforms also greatly exacerbated the major
social divisions in Peruvian society. By removing the ideological cover of
developmentalism, neoliberalism required much more open coercion. In

some countries like Guatemala and Bolivia these reforms amounted to neoliberal multiculturalism, a hegemonic form of exploitation through (selective) inclusion. In Peru, however, the central state variously retrenched indigenous racialization in order to advance neoliberalization, up to the point of marshaling a primitive fear of natives to leverage authoritarian state powers.

While concerned with the longer-term and contested construction of decentralized despotism, this book primarily focuses on the how developmentalism and neoliberalism unfurled in the village of Huaytabamba, and identifying how the enabling institutional and cultural practices perpetuated a system of racialized indirect rule.

BOOK OVERVIEW

The remainder of this book intertwines a narrative of village politics with an explanation of the social dynamics enabling them. Chapter 2 details the historic emergence, transformation, and continual renewal of racialized indirect rule from conquest to 1980. This chapter argues that, rather than through path dependency, preserving this largely aristocratic system required tremendous resources and incurred considerable costs, such as contributing to Peru's military routing and loss of rich nitrate deposits to Chile in the nineteenth century. Despite creative and diverse native resistance, inter-elite conflict, and large-scale social transformations like the transition to a liberal state, mestizaje, and ostensibly pro-native agrarian reform, the ruling group regularly poured tremendous resources into predicating their own advantages on indigenous disenfranchisement. Through a narration of the contentious politics across the centuries, this chapter shows how the specifics of the Indian Question regularly changed as did the means of answering it. But the general answer preserved the key aspects of indirect rule: an authoritarian but conflicted local leadership dependent upon fracturing and exploiting native peoples.

Chapter 3 spells out the different elements of the developmentalist incarnation of indirect rule through narrating how Damian employed multiple development projects to generate a cycle of increased villager exploitation until he "stripped all the community members of their money." This chapter starts with a brief account of two large Damian-brokered projects that promised to increase village lands by 30 percent and triple local cattle holdings. After years of villagers investing money and labor, once "they sold their horses, cows, pigs, everything in order to supply money and have [the project] finally come out," the projects finally ended with Damian disappearing with all their funds.

With Damian's departure, villagers "lost all trust in the authorities then and . . . they didn't even want to work together in the fields so the [later] authorities couldn't do anything." Over the next four years, however, new leaders emerging from the local Evangelical church successfully revitalized comunidad institutions and ethnically based proclivities towards mutuality. Chapter 4 details the rise, characteristics, and village leadership of the local church, specifically focusing on the particularly Evangelical means through which the church revitalized the community, altering but not fully overcoming the dynamics of racialized indirect rule.

Chapters 5 and 6 address the Huaytabamba privatization struggle that began at the height of Evangelical domination. They explore the myriad actions of the pro-privatization group, the countermoves of the pro-community faction, the interactions with urban institutions, and how these engaged with the legacy of indirect rule. As the privatization battle escalated, it infected all aspects of village life, polarizing them into dysfunction. Chapter 6 finishes by spelling out the implications of the eventual triumph of the privatizers, and the new authoritarian character this brought to indirect rule.

The concluding chapter reconsiders Huaytabamba's developmentalist exploitation and its neoliberal authoritarianism as two different regimes of racialized indirect rule. Initially, this enables an analysis of how different globalizing forces leverage racism to achieve their localized outcomes, and therein alter the nature of racialized rule. Considering these together, I next draw the larger implications of these regimes for better understanding the racialized nature of the global political economy, noting that neoliberalism's heightened emphasis on extractive logics only makes colonial divisions more empowered and important. All in all, racial analyses need to assume much greater primacy for understanding social dynamics in Latin America (and beyond), and this book provides some key routes for doing so.

BOOK COVER

I never could have learned so much about Huaytabamba except through the help of my incredible research assistant, Edilberto Jimenez Quispe, whose artwork graces the cover of this book. I had gotten to know Edilberto through his work with local NGOs. He was from a famous family of artists from another part of the department. But he had worked several times in Huaytabamba, with villagers knowing and liking him. I hired Edilberto once villagers and I began discussing more complex issues. Simply having another person in the field, who understood the research endeavor, proved a tremendous boon. Moreover, I was happy to see Edilberto as wiped out by fieldwork as I was. But Edilberto was extremely talented at conducting interviews. He became intimate with the local issues I had been gathering information on. And his Spanish-Quechua bilingual skills fully enabled him to conduct penetrating interviews in which villagers could more fully express themselves.

He had recently honed his skills through working with the Truth Commission and other groups to document the violence of the recent civil war. This including toiling through the remote area of Chungui that had experienced such a "limitless violence" that the Commission itself refused to enter for the lawlessness that still reigned. Edilberto developed his artistic pictures to document these atrocities, adapting to two-dimensional pen and ink the three-dimensional form of *retablos* of which he and his family were renowned. Retablo literally means altarpiece, but has evolved from its syncretistic origins depicting local gods cum Catholic saints to depict a wide and frequently subtle picture of various social realities, generally amounting to a folk idealization of rural life. Edilberto's mixture of this comic styling with the excessively grim (scenes of torture, mass murder, and other) horrors of civil war portrays the kind of dark humor through which many Andeans both face and live through the hardships of their lives. I am eternally grateful that he agreed to turn his artistic eye to the issues of this book.

NOTES

1. All names, including that of the village, are pseudonyms.
2. See, for instance, the otherwise excellent Poole (1994) and Heilmann (2010).

TWO

Historical Arc

Centuries/Sentries of Contested Racism

Towards establishing a more systemic understanding of the racial domination of native peoples, this chapter offers a retelling of Peruvian history with race at its core.[1] Such a broad sweep of history is necessarily provisional and cannot hope to account for variation. While later studies can address these issues, this chapter simply aims to demonstrate the historical tenacity of indirect rule and its subordination of indigenous peoples. Continually facing native pressures for more inclusive forms of governance in a radically diverse set of historical circumstances, the dominant sectors have consistently refashioned indirect rule to fit the changing landscape, providing it with innovative resources rather than diminishing or even dismantling it. The specifics of the Indian Question have changed dramatically through the centuries. But the dominant groups have persisted in asking it and providing it with new answers, consistently reinforcing the conflicted sentries that straddle the bifurcated state.

I argue that once the Spanish instituted the notion of racial superiority within the organization of society, maintaining racial dominance mainly required participating in the institutions as they were designed, and bolstering them in times of crisis. Conquest and colonization deliberately created a complex institutional structure through which to maintain racial domination. Once the society was racialized, racial subordination mainly occurred through the routine practices and organization of the core social institutions. Racial domination was the normal, desired, and easiest outcome of the way society had become organized. And racist ideologies arose as justifications for the perpetuation of this unequal system. But crises have wracked Peruvian history. These provided many opportunities to reshape society in much more inclusive ways. The tre-

19

mendous scale and diversity of resources the dominant groups spent to close these opportunities demonstrates their great dedication to maintaining the racial hierarchy.

CONQUEST AND COLONIZATION, 1532–1820

While conquest established the very racist economy of plunder, the later colonial project actually intensified racialized rule. More specifically, conquest established the rough parameters of indirect rule that the Spanish accelerated in response to crises arising from a diversifying society. Grossly racist acts abounded under early Spanish rule, such as slaughtering, enslaving, and hunting natives with dogs for sport, a sadism Gonzalo Portocarrero (2007) regards as still influencing contemporary social relations. Institutionally, the Spanish Crown granted lordly oversight to Spanish settlers. These *encomiendas* made up the backbone of the economy of plunder, with Spanish *encomenderos* granting indigenous villages corporate control over a set piece of land in exchange for tribute (Klarén 2000, 42; Wolf 1982; Wolf and Hansen 1972). Encomenderos centralized power through town councils, or *cabildos*, which provided the separate and authoritarian administrative apparatus necessary for indirect rule. A modified cabildo that still lacks any means of accountability continues to govern rural communities. Impunity and random violence characterized encomienda rule, making these figures reviled by the native populations, even inspiring massive gifts to the Crown to eliminate the encomienda system.

While bloody and exploitative, the Indian Question at this time actually concerned the relatively simple issue of placing the new powers on top of existing systems in order to exact as much native wealth as possible and minimize discontent. Indeed, this early system relied almost exclusively on preserving the native socioeconomic system. As Steve J. Stern (1992, 44) describes it, "the colonials remained foreign, extraneous elements superimposed on an autonomous economy in which they served little purpose." In particular, the colonials relied upon reciprocal relations with local native lords (*curacas*) who controlled native labor and resources. The most successful encomenderos lavished gifts upon their curacas to assure both the continual flow of tribute and the safeguarding of their own positions. While many abuses occurred, the curacas, in turn, could legitimate their vaunted position as safeguarding native society, and even present themselves as liberators from Incan rule (Stern 1992; Klarén 2000, 45). Many native groups thereby entered into strategic—if uneasy—alliances with the colonials in order to preserve the integrity of local society and gain protection from rivals. From the start, though, highly powerful intermediaries maintained the social system largely through the back and forth flow of patronage. Little challenged by their

Spanish patróns or native constituents, contradictory impulses between protection and exploitation still characterized curaca rule.

While the initial conquest may have happened through the Spanish "taking advantage of [Indian] differences, whipping one against the other," the means of domination were subtler (Portocarrero 2007, 57). The Spanish ability to quickly divide the natives and rule them through the local native aristocracy was due in large part to pre-existing conditions and the nature of Incan rule. The Inca partially dominated through exacerbating the divides between different ethnic groups and vaunting the local curacas to high positions of wealth and status (Spalding 1970, 655). When the Spanish removed the Inca, most natives gladly refocused their organization around their local group, particularly as their complex networks of kinship ties were the primary means of accessing resources (Spalding 1970, 653). Under these conditions, alliance with the Spaniards became a route to social mobility due to the removal of Incan restrictions and the establishment of the new religious and political organizations through which the colonials sought to exercise control (Spalding 1970, 656).

These overlapping Spanish and native routes to wealth and status began splintering native society, generating new sources for conflicting alliances and interests (Spalding 1970). The Spanish also exacerbated incipient class differentiation inherent in Andean social relations, and deepened ethnic rivalries, such as for the spoils of Incan imperial warehouses and other resources. While the native cultures and economies preserved their overall integrity, internal discord grew, as did native recourse to Spanish intervention to solve local ethnic problems (Stern 1992). But the central governing dynamic of early colonialism hung on the contradictory position of the curaca who, backed by Spanish coercive power, preserved local society by providing a steady stream of labor and tribute to the colonists.

The Toledo Reforms

By the 1560s, however, Spanish rule faced serious crisis. As the white population grew and diversified, the shared desire to exploit native labor exacerbated competition and rivalry amongst colonials, especially as they lacked the institutional capacity to directly recruit labor. Rather than building the infrastructure for coordinated policy implementation, however, they persisted in their self-splintering strategies of relying on their own patronage networks, increasing their dependence on and exploitation of the curacas. At the same time, colonials faced deteriorating economic output at the silver mines in Potosí, increased demand for labor from the entire mining sector, heightened threats of rebellion from the neo-Incas, and the debility of the encomienda system, inspiring ever greater extractions from the native populations.

In the countryside, meanwhile, the fracturing of ethnic relations increasingly made colonists the final arbiters in local disputes. Concomitant with this rise in political power and legitimacy, the Spanish continually increased their demands for labor and tribute. But such wringing eroded the local system of control. In particular, it dramatically sharpened the contradictory role of the curaca middlemen, threatening to turn them into agents of colonialism. The increased penetration and demands of Spanish authority undermined the motivation for natives to make strategic, autonomy-preserving alliances with the colonists. Instead, Spanish desires to consolidate natives into a more fully racialized Indian group for the strict end of colonial extraction became increasingly evident. Under these circumstances, appeasing Europeans came to resemble participating in one's own destruction much more than preserving native autonomy.

The overall colonial strategy still centered on fracturing native society in order to make them exploitable on the cheap, that is, without building a distinct colonial infrastructure requiring coordination from a dysfunctional colonial society. The Spanish grasped ever harder onto this model even as it unfrayed. Among other things, this meant the preservation of generally self-sustaining and autonomous indigenous spheres that enabled natives to construct widespread anti-colonial movements in the midst of colonial rule itself. Thus, an array of native groups responded in diverse manners to the heart of the matter: Spanish insistence on increased wealth extraction. Thousands joined Taki Onqoy, the dancing sickness movement that promised a total overthrow of the Spanish and their God through Andean ethnic unification. New rebellions sprouted up among the centrally located Huancas. The neo-Inca state in the jungle city of Vitcos continued regular guerilla incursions into Spanish areas. On a smaller but more widespread level, multiple forms of subversion accelerated encomienda decline, Indians creating many ways to undercut colonial obligations of wealth and labor. Rather than tempering extractive demands, however, the Spanish responded by dramatically scaling up racialization. This not only severely exacerbated the multiple systemic problems, it also cut into the revenues flowing to the Spanish throne.

Responding to this severe crisis and the obvious inability of colonials to address it, the Crown dispatched a new Viceroy to impose a dramatic remaking of social relations. Rather than somehow negotiating a more humane social system (of which there were several contemporary models), the Toledo reforms of the 1570s refashioned the Indian Question to ask how colonial society could increasingly penetrate and exploit the Indian Republic to eventually break the back of the native economy and have its labor directly serve the Spanish.

To accomplish this, Toledo had to work on multiple fronts simultaneously, confronting the natives militaristically, religiously, politically, and socially. The reforms sought a radical transformation of the native populations so they could be systematically administered and exploited by the Spanish while quelling resources for rebellion. He also had to discipline the colonial upper classes, aligning their interests into a civil society designed for native exploitation. This was a civil society largely forced upon the citizenry through strong state action. Toledo explicitly set it up in direct conflict with natives, predicated upon their disenfranchisement, and with the explicit goal of extracting as much labor and wealth as possible. In other words, the wellbeing of colonial society came to depend on the undermining of native society. Herein Toledo established the racial legacy of institutionalized segregation: distinct governing bodies for the colonials for the purpose of exploiting the distinct Indian institutions that engendered dependence. Perhaps not surprisingly, the architect of these plans, Juan de Matienzo, justified them in unabashedly racist ways, finding that even after the decades of extracting huge quantities of material wealth, the natives still owed the Spanish for the gift of Christian civilization (Stern 1992).

Toledo unleashed a huge military expedition against the neo-Incas culminating finally in the public execution of the last Inca, Tupac Amaru, thereby completing the conquest project. Inquisition-like religious purges brutally rooted out the leaders and practices upon which millenarian uprisings had been based (Stern 1992). The Crown eliminated the reviled encomenderos but replaced them with state functionaries called *corregidores de Indios* who enjoyed much more direct control over and ability to exploit native populations, more systematically extracting tribute and labor recruitment (*mita*). To further profit from and offset the onerous costs of their office, the corregidores introduced the illegal but widespread forced sale of merchandise (*reparto*) upon natives. Corregidores also frequently usurped Indian reserves (*caja de comunidad*) for their own enrichment, many seeing the office as a way to enhance their own social and economic positions.

The reforms consolidated the patrimonial nature of the state with increased tributes enabling the Crown to appoint and maintain loyal and worthy subjects (Klarén 2000, 64). Additionally, corregidores could newly grant lands, thereby giving rise to the haciendas which would dominate social relations in subsequent centuries. As these reforms came to predominate, the 1633 move to sell imperial offices caused government corruption to become endemic, establishing the long-enduring practice of using such offices for personal gain rather than disinterested public service (Klarén 2000, 89).

As a result of the reforms, overall native wellbeing deteriorated precipitously. To wrest control of the natives from the curacas—who had become more demanding and less willing to deliver tribute and labor—the reforms forcibly relocated indigenous populations onto concentrated landholdings. As one of the most brutal parts of the reforms, relocation to these reductions truncated traditional dispersed settlements, massively displaced the native populations, and generally uprooted them from the physical terrain through which they reproduced their local cultures. Natives lived in much more squalid conditions, reliant on external labor markets for their reproduction, and were much more susceptible to pathogens, both because of their population concentration and their deteriorated living conditions. Malnutrition and famine spread. While earlier alliances with the Spanish may have staved off the demographic collapse witnessed in other parts of Latin America, Toledo's breaking of native self-sufficiency now brought population collapse to the Andes.

Instead of creating a colonist-staffed colonial apparatus for ruling the natives directly, the corregidor system remade the native power structure so it was dependent on the benevolence of the state and served the interests of the colonial authorities (Stern 1992, 92). Toledo set up Indian cabildos and other official positions that received direct remuneration, creating a privileged native managerial class dependent upon reproducing the institutional arrangements of the colonial regime. These new native authorities undermined the demands of the troublesome curacas, and their ability to marshal native labor to serve these demands. In this way, the new corregidor system revitalized the position of the largely authoritarian intermediary upon whom indirect rule depends, creating a new group more willing and able to serve Crown interests, while pushing the curacas towards more market forms of interchange rather than the kin networks of reciprocity through which they controlled native labor (Spalding 1973; Stern 1992).

The major contradiction of the Toledo reform era was that it sought to dramatically increase the amount of native labor available for Spanish exploitation at the same time that it eroded the ability of native labor to reproduce itself. But several other contradictions undergirded this central dynamic. While the Toledo reforms largely destroyed the basis of the self-reproducing native economy, they did not aim at undercutting native self-sufficiency. The reforms were designed primarily to redirect native labor from the Indian to the colonial economy, preserving native land access because viable local food production enabled the Spanish to pay wages well below the costs of labor reproduction. Indeed, most colonial prosperity was due to this ability to super-exploit native labor (Stern 1992).

Nevertheless, much of the new system undermined native self-sufficiency. While the viability of the colonial economy rested on native subsistence production, individual colonists profited to the extent they exploited native labor, thereby lacking incentives to guarantee native labor reproduction. Indeed, some figures became extremely wealthy through famously overworking their labor allotments. The monetization of tribute and the new labor draft system dramatically increased the capacity and geographic reach of labor conscription. But these practices also cut into the physical and social resources necessary for native self-sufficiency.

With locals either regularly drafted or migrating away as rootless *forest-eros*, combined with the rise in epidemics and disease, local food systems suffered major setbacks. The slowness of the erosion of local self-suffi-ciency, however, enabled natives to take advantage of rising commercial activities offered by a diversifying economy. In this way, many groups amassed wealth and became largely independent, and therefore much less willing to participate in labor conscription—though these Indian cof-fers made lucrative targets for rapacious corregidores.

Despite the draconian changes, natives still managed to find innova-tive means of resistance. These included competing commercially with the Spanish, filing lawsuits, and attempting to form closed corporate communities in areas of little interest to the colonists (Grieshaber 1979; Stern 1992). Nevertheless, as indicative of a system of indirect rule, with these new tools also used against other natives, they provided more local-ized splintering effects than real challenges to the system of racial domi-nation. The system therein usurped the native culture of resistance to insulate the dominant group from enacting more inclusive changes. Rath-er than being passive victims of European racism, or agents able to trans-form the entire colonial system, natives found creative ways of challeng-ing and thereby shaping the colonial system so as to address some of their own interests. The point made by Stern, though, is that challenging the Europeans through the system made the overall system stronger and the natives much less able to overcome colonial domination as a whole.

In sum, the Toledo reforms were a bald coercive act, using multiple fronts of brute force to break the back of the native economy and recon-struct indigenous societies to more directly fit the diversified needs of the colonists. The multipronged attack on native societies transformed na-tives from independent sociocultural groups into splintered dependents of colonial society. Through this coercion, though, the state established a revamped institutional structure of indirect rule that could stably main-tain Spanish domination. After the dismantling of the key resources of native independence, the reforms reinvigorated the institutional segrega-tion, conflicted leadership, and localized fracturing central to racialized indirect rule. Post-reform, the colonists regularly resorted to various forms of violence. But these actions were much more strategic than in the earlier period, and largely served to keep the institutional structure run-ning rather than the much more ambitious action of transforming it. All told, the reforms poured tremendous resources into honing the system of indirect rule, finally completely racialized the native peoples, so that "[b]y the end of the sixteenth century, in fact if not in law, native re-sources in land, labor, and goods were regarded as a reservoir upon which members of Spanish society could draw with relative impunity" (Spalding 1973, 589). That is, Toledo transformed the natives from di-verse, largely independent groups into a single group of Indians marked for full and open exploitation.

In the post-reform social reality, the new Indian Question came to ask: as labor supplies diminish, both from death and from out-migration as foresteros, how can colonials maintain access to pools of powerless workers? The hacienda, existing alongside Indian villages and in direct cahoots with the state, emerged as the most robust answer. Haciendas were relatively small landed estates producing largely for internal markets in Peruvian cities. But this system formally introduced the figure of the European racial exception living (some of the time) amidst Indian territory for the purpose of social control and surplus extraction. As with other feudal-like social arrangements, these exceptions enjoyed the clearly spelled out special rights and privileges conferred to the landed aristocracy, while clearly exempted from any of the demeaning obligations imposed on the native populations of the same geographic area.

Hacienda survival depended upon (1) paying below subsistence wages to a self-sustaining labor population that (2) was coerced to work on the haciendas (Spalding 1975, 116). A captured population on the haciendas, mainly of foresteros, provided some labor, and helped curtail the native strategy of flight. But the self-sustaining aspects of villages provided the most cost-effective and flexible answer. The state therefore protected the much altered traditional native landholdings as a reservoir of cheap labor, run by the new native authorities, such as privileged hacienda workers like *caporales*, whose social position increased markedly simply through representing the threat of violent state power. That is, the state deliberately, and in direct alignment with highland power holders, institutionalized a space for natives so colonials could exploit Indians as Indians—rather than directly incorporating them as citizens. Further, many curacas became hacienda owners directly vested in maintaining the system of Indian exploitation, truncating this possible source of powerful discontent. And to stave off competition from market-integrated Indians, the state forcibly reduced native landholdings and thereby the capacity to produce a surplus (Spalding 1975; Grieshaber 1979).

Andean Insurrection

By the eighteenth century, exploitative pressures within this system increased dramatically, especially with the new Spanish Bourbon monarchy siphoning more American resources in an attempt to revitalize Spain's world position. Charles III, the new Spanish king, pressed corregidors to dramatically increase Indian tax collections, amounting to the pillaging of rural society (Klarén 2000, 120). But these new policies also alienated hacienda owners and other intermediary commercial interests by absorbing a much greater share of Indian surplus exclusively for the Crown. And the reforms angered the *criollo* (American-born white) population by reasserting the authority of the Iberian born. The extreme and fairly naked exploitation tapped into much of the general Indian peasant discontent about colonial relations. Thus, all strata of society shared hostility towards the new Crown policies. This included the intermediaries who acted for and largely defined colonial rule over Indians. Their traditional dilemma between exploiting and protecting their native wards therein became largely resolved in favor of the Indian. Such brokers began using their privileged positions to serve Indian interests. Revolts erupted throughout the Sierra.

In contrast to the Crown policy of redoubling exploitative relations, several new ideas emerged from the Andean populations. Many created small strategies that exploited the contradictions of the system. On a larger scale, some groups, such as those led by Juan Santos Atahualpa, established their own small nations in more remote and easier to defend areas (Mallon 1983). But Tupac Amaru II, the leader of the Great Rebellion (1780–1781), the most notorious event of these times, was clearly influenced by ideas about a much more inclusive society based on Enlightenment thought filtered through idealized versions of Andean nationalism (Flores Galindo 1988). And notions of undoing Spanish colonialism had swelled his ranks with the general Indian populace—at the same time that it alienated those natives enjoying some relative privilege from the system (Garrett 2004). The Great Rebellion cost the lives of nearly ten percent of the native population and "opened an enormous breach between Indian and Spanish Peru that has still not been closed more than 200 years later" (Klaren 2000, 121). The Spanish tried to ensure against any future mass Indian uprisings, unleashing a reign of terror upon sympathizers, including killing every fifth able-bodied male in some villages (the *quintado*).

As native political power plummeted and the Crown now needed more Indian tribute to pay the costs of the Rebellion and Spain's wars in Europe, the new *subdelegado* system, replacing the hated *corregidores*, generally intensified exploitation. With the 1787 abolition of the curacas, the "indigenous aristocracy withered, losing whatever status and position it had held as 'intermediaries' in the colonial order," making natives ever more vulnerable while increasing their homogenization as a racialized but splintered Indian underclass (Klarén 2000, 120). While the colonials preserved native areas as reservoirs of cheap labor, local authorities became much more dependent upon exterior support, and less able to leverage more favorable relations. The European-identifying hacendados became increasingly more central and powerful in rural indigenous society. To maintain the bifurcated state, racial distinctions became more pronounced in the countryside, rural Europeans enjoying titles, such as *vecino notable*, which distinguished them as urban citizens amidst a geography of Crown subjects. The more immediate dependence on the hacendados, however, enabled the colonial economy to diversify and take greater advantage of the new international trade opportunities arising from British industrial ascendancy (particularly in wool).

INDEPENDENCE, PACIFIC, AND CIVIL WARS, 1820–1895

The early nineteenth-century Latin American independence movements, of which the Peruvian elite was a reluctant part, presented several opportunities to end racialized indirect rule. Foremost, they toppled the colonial state and established a new system based on Enlightenment liberal inclusiveness. In their military actions, the elites relied significantly on natives, making Indians central players in the establishment of the newly independent state, and giving them some power and social connections through which to express their ideas about creating a more inclusive society. More importantly, these ideas meshed with criollo critiques of the colonial state and modern notions of popular sovereignty upon which the new state was founded (Thurner 1995; 1997).

But Independence instead revitalized the system. In fact, indigenous racial domination actually intensified to such an extent that some native groups struggled to reinstate the more protective colonial state form (Thurner 1995; 1997). Independence remade the dominant group, and criollos reasserted their control of the state. With the fall of the beleaguered colonial state and the disorganization of the wars of Independence, however, the Indian Question changed to ask: how can a liberal state, impoverished by history and war, and dependent upon a colonial Indian head tax (newly coined the *contribución indígena*) for forty percent of the national budget, exercise control of the territory?

Privatization provided the answer. The state privatized native landholdings, resulting in the massive growth of haciendas as a private means to control native labor, formerly achieved through direct state intervention (Spalding 1975). But, more importantly, the state privatized much of its coercive force in the hands of the post-war emergent highland strongmen (gamonales and caudillos), scattering these powers to those landholders who could muster sufficient personal and military power to hold them. Economically, beyond seizing natives' lands and forcing their labor, gamonales eventually fully privatized the contribución in 1854 once the central state replaced this income with exporting rich coastal guano reserves. The criollo state therein answered the new Indian Question with a fractious compromise with highland elites, granting them carte blanche powers over natives in exchange for social control and maintaining the flow of Indian tribute. For natives, the liberal state meant the consolidation of European-identifying citizens into the authoritarian positions, ruling colonized subjects now stripped of protections either from an indigenous aristocracy or colonial forms of appeal.

As in previous eras, these new figures ruled through the traditional "webs of clientage and modes of coercion that penetrated deep into post-independence Indian society" (Klarén 2000, 137–138). They used their power to perpetuate the racial division of labor that relegated natives to the most grueling agricultural work (Appelbaum et al. 2003). Contrary to a more generous reconstruction of caudillismo (Walker 1999), the ascendant gamonales followed their predecessors in stunting economic differentiation in order to keep natives unskilled and dependent upon paternalistic largess. Indeed, any kind of market differentiation and rise of a native entrepreneurial class occurred only in the few areas like the Mantaro valley where haciendas did not exist but lands were productive (Mallon 1983). But even in these areas differentiation was limited, with the commercial intermediary figures benefiting from the racial division of labor and using various means for its retrenchment.

Under these conditions, disorder reigned amidst bald power plays, the presidency changing hands twenty-three times in as many years, 1821–1845. The corruption and disorder of the Peruvian state squandered the fortunes of the guano boom (1840–1880), and led to Peru's routing by invading Chilean forces in the War of the Pacific (1879–1883) in which Peru lost its rich nitrate producing areas (Bonilla 1974; Gootenberg 1991). The disparate European gamonales rallied indigenous troops; but they foundered in front of the organized Chilean army who occupied Lima and won tremendous peace concessions.

Civil war filled the vacuum until one of the warring generals, Andrés Avelino Cáceres, emerged triumphant by making promises of inclusion to the indigenous populations who famously rallied to his cause. Cáceres, however, reneged on his promises of infrastructure and the elimination of colonial taxes, and instead reinstated the aristocratic state, granting the traditional means of social control to the landlords on whom he depended. Indeed, Cáceres famously brought to heel the nationalist aspirations of some former indigenous allies through such means as slaughter, torture, and public execution (Mallon 1995; Thurner 1997).

NATION FORMATION AND THE THIRD RACE, 1895–1968

The fractious state of the nineteenth century presented coastal elites with a new question in the twentieth. How can they cohere the nation while maintaining the aristocratic system conferring highly unequal privileges? This national question entailed a new Indian Question: how can the coastal elites create a purportedly all-inclusive Peruvian identity without empowering the native nationalist aspirations that would threaten elites' gamonal allies? Through complex, multifaceted struggles, the imperfect answer became: mestizaje.

As with much of the rest of the Americas, the Peruvian elite subscribed to Spencerian ideas of inherent white racial superiority, particularly as manifest by the complexity of industrialized society. To improve their own society, then, the Peruvian elite attempted to whiten the population through promoting immigration from northern Europe. Failing this, they settled for a strategy of racial improvement through intermixture between Europeans and indigenous populations.

This proved a more inclusive strategy than the previous policies based on ideas of pure whites, inherently inferior Indians, and degeneration through miscegenation. While relenting on notions of racial purity, for elites this move addressed several key threats to their power. Most importantly, it dampened discontent through a strategic inclusion of select popular sectors. Elites could then legitimately draw on these labor pools for the more dynamic, non-agricultural costal enterprises. The labor market therein began to bifurcate between these mestizo jobs and their Indian counterpart still highly racialized as undifferentiated brute manual labor. Mestizo inclusion therein divided popular sectors against themselves.

Elites retrenched Indian racial domination by placing the once highly marginalized "worst of both worlds" cholos and mestizos above natives in the racial hierarchy. Culturally, Indians faced a new form of racism as their route to political inclusion now came through assimilation to mestizo practices. Finally, as mestizaje involved denial of the indigenous parts of the racial mixture, the newly enfranchised middle stratum served as a strong racial police. Racial contestation riddled mestizos, forcing them to compete for resources through asserting their less Indian-ness within their endless internal gradations, and giving rise to expressions like "you let the Indian out of you." Thus, mestizo inclusion meant buffering for the white elites, retrenched marginalization for Indians, and internal discord for mestizos.

For the most part, the Aristocratic Republic of 1895–1919 managed its oxymoronic contradictions through a tight alliance with international capital—though at the expense of the tremendous penetration of foreign corporations (Thorp and Bertram 1978; Burga and Flores-Galindo 1987). By the twentieth century, however, the coastal elites' own actions created inroads for competing demands on the state: from other elites, from the rising middle class, and from multiple popular groups. Preeminently, an increasing coastal economic dynamism in both agro-exports and manufacturing altered the sociopolitical landscape. Highland residents increasingly abandoned gamonal rule and its stifling of economic differentiation. Lured by higher wages on the coast, they became the new, mestizo-associated urban masses. In coastal cities, a new working-class culture emerged that enabled mobilization based on class interests and identity (Stokes 1995). Working class demands employed European anarcho-syndicalist frameworks, but also followed the deep forestero tradition of asserting a non-Indian, and therefore non-servile, position. With the general strike of 1919, workers became a political force, with labor unrest seething throughout the century in the cities, coastal plantations, and Andean mines alike (Klarén 2000, 271).

In the highlands, the native populations engaged in passive resistance but also seized lands when possible. With the dramatic growth of wool exports to Great Britain, gamonales grabbed more lands and monopolized markets, increasing the economic pressures on natives in attempts to maintain their paternalist authoritarian control (Spalding 1975; Collins 1988). Natives, however, found allies among the emerging working class and coastal elite. In the 1920s, Augusto Leguía, a coastal capitalist and sugar baron, used populist working-class appeals to ride to power. Leguía similarly challenged gamonal power by asserting the central state as the new arbiter between peasants and landlords. He frequently sided with natives to appeal to the growing pro-native *indigenismo* sentiments among the urban middle and working classes. These direct ties to external allies enabled broad native coalitions, such as the Comité Central pro-Derecho Indigena "Tawantinsuyo," to express and fight for large-scale reformist agendas that meshed well with the liberal nationalism of the day (de la Cadena 2000).

Such catering to the popular classes, however, soon divided the elites, many of whom saw popular mobilizations as threatening their interests—not to mention soiling the extant political culture. Leguía was forced from office. Labor militancy, finding its strongest voice in the APRA (American Popular Revolutionary Alliance) party, experienced heavy repression and the exile of its leaders. And, as native mobilizations in the sierra built momentum towards a serious mass movement, the state and its agents unleashed ruthless repression, in Puno alone killing two thousand peasants. And the military repeatedly took direct control of the state.

The cycles of military and civilian rule in the twentieth century largely resulted from the coastal elite attempting to retain their oligarchic interests in the face of rising popular movements and their capitalist need for some social stability. Direct repression proved a powerful tool for reshaping popular opposition to better fit these goals. By and large, however, the elite aimed their forces of compromise at workers, particularly in the coastal cities. This amounted to a breaking and remaking of the workers' movement so as to conform to the racial division of labor. First, they seriously hobbled the labor movement. In 1945 they moderated the radical worker agenda by getting APRA leaders to sign a moderate reformist agenda in exchange for legitimacy. This gave a seat at the table to an ambivalent party leadership that largely failed to represent most workers' demands, while intensifying internal party divisions. Elites also began shaping labor as mestizo by reforming their failed whitening policy of importing European workers into popular education programs explicitly aimed at inclusion through assimilation. And new scientifically justified ideas about the inherent inferiority of natives invigorated the contradictory mestizo condemnation of the backward Indian with whom they shared blood (Klarén 2000).

So refashioned, any genuine affinity between native peasant interests and those of urban middle and working classes became significantly eroded. State mestizaje created a strong association between mestizaje and urban citizenship, meaning that people had to continuously distinguish themselves as non-Indian in order to partake in worker gains. Natives therein became beholden to a group whose own interests entailed indigenous subjugation. At the same time, indigenismo no longer embraced or even dialogued with native nationalism, but rather mimicked gamonal paternalism in wanting to grant rights to Indians only when "made more productive and healthier" (Bourricaud 1968, 377). Rural APRA activities, while implicitly favoring peasants, was extremely limited as any major activity amounted to a challenge to the seigniorial system of the gamonales and thus a violation of the APRA promise of moderation, further cementing the labor movement as an urban-based mestizo phenomenon.

Rather than ushering a new inclusivity, this national period represented a resolution of elite conflicts through the reassertion of coastal criollo authority, empowered by new sources of wealth and guarded by the conflicted mestizos. For natives, state mestizaje further entrenched gamonal highland rule by linking it culturally to the emergent urban mestizo interests. While repression reigned in both the coast and highlands, any institutional reconciliation happened only on the coast and in explicitly mestizo assimilationist ways. Any worker rights came through mestizaje. Race thereby once again pitted mutual interests against each other. Overall, mestizaje newly answered the Indian Question by creating an entire middle stratum barrier to native enfranchisement that crossed the various mestizo classes and interests, and that was embedded in the internally conflicted and fluctuating mestizo urban culture.

THE AGRARIAN REFORM, 1969–1980

Despite marginalization behind the barriers of the mestizo culture and gamonal despotism, native resistance continued and increased. By the 1950s and 1960s, land occupations accelerated to the point that land reform became a regularly contended issue on the national stage. The reforms of the military government of General Juan Velasco (1968–1975) finally addressed these head on. But they altered rather than overcame the system of rural despotism. The powerful simply created new means to dominate locally, such as through staffing the agrarian reform offices or monopolizing key local resources, such as transportation and money lending (van den Berghe and Primov 1977; Collins 1988; Lagos 1994; Poole 1994; Renique 1994; Zimmerer 1996). The new political entity of "peasant communities" granted natives political autonomy but strangled these economically by forcing all resource acquisition through the old clientelist networks. In all, "the revolutionary armed forces reproduced the traditional top-down vertical structures of domination of the oligarchic period" (Drinot 2006, 19).

The military government, however, did refashion the tools of patronage into the productive sphere, qualitatively changing the type of patronage and the ideology rationalizing the rural-urban connections. Under the ideological banner of "the land for those who work it," the new state patrón focused on issues of farming infrastructure and markets. The greatest promised patronage was the land itself; but the actual redistribution provided few positive results (Kay 1981; Mallon 1998; Drinot 2006). From this point forward, however, the guise of the paternalist control of the countryside fell under the banner of "development" and became almost exclusively economic. The splintering effects of mestizaje intensified as mestizos came to embody developmentalism, mestizos occupying all of the urban development agencies upon which rural villagers depended for resources. The superior position of the patrón was therein reconstructed to promise improved material wellbeing for the populace.

But the industrialization policies of subsidizing urban areas with cheap rural food created some of the greatest racial divides. The very wellbeing of the urban mestizo workers depended upon the price controls undercutting rural native incomes. Further, these arrangements, coupled with the overall growth of the highland populations, consolidated the semi-proletarian nature of most native labor (Mallon 1983; Thiele 1991). The new peasants worked at below subsistence wages, subsidized by farming small land plots—a similar reproductive situation to that established by Toledo four hundred years previously.

Not only did this new focus on development, then, make people's economic wellbeing track with their race, but it enhanced the earlier predication of mestizo privileges upon native subordination, now spelled out in clear economic terms. Under these conditions urbanization flourished, with peasants fleeing the stagnant rural economy in favor of the dynamic subsidized cities. Demographically, Nelson Manrique (1999) explains a massive downturn in indigenous numbers, far outstripping birth, death, and intermixture rates, due primarily to urban growth on the coast at the expense of the rural sierra. People changed their race by moving from the countryside to the city. State mestizaje clearly accelerated under Velasco.

The new policies also reinvigorated the atomization of native political engagement while obscuring the racialized content of the policies. Explicitly reformist in character, by legally transforming natives from "Indians" to "peasants" the government tossed out natives' patrimonial land rights, replacing them with class rights to work the soil. This successfully reoriented the struggle away from any indigenous liberatory ideas of transforming the state, and towards the exploitative atrocities of local landlords. The state therein became the peasants' champion, removing the rapacious gamonales, but severely limiting reforms to the highly local. The "peasant-ization" of natives also enhanced the mestizaje dialogue of equating racism with speaking about racial differences (Callirgos 1993). As in other countries, this "color-blind" perspective helped perpetuate the racial inequalities generated by the new policies (Guinier and Torres 2002).

After the 1980 departure of the military governments, each successive administration left its particular marks on the countryside, recasting the content of race relations, but keeping the structural divisions largely intact. The following chapters pick up this story as it unfolds in the community of Huaytabamba, detailing the actions and institutions through which villagers navigated their way through developmentalism and into neoliberalism.

NOTE

1. This chapter is a revised version of Scarritt (2012).

THREE

Exploiting through the Guise of Helping

"Everything was fine until we got the tractor," don Miguel explained to me during a break from working in his field.[1] And, indeed, everyone kept complaining about the tractor. It took me a long time to listen, though, because the only big story about a tractor in this farming village was that they had one and no other community did. And villagers freely admitted that tractors do better work faster. Without a tractor, turning over the soil required coaxing a yoked bull across precipitous terrain, or the brutal labor intensity of people in lines swinging picks in unison and ripping out the turf. Harvesting without a tractor also involved back-breaking work. Indeed, on one particularly steep field, once the tractor pulled potatoes from the ground they rolled down the hill into waiting hands. The tractor also made money for the village when they hired it out to neighboring towns.

Looking up to the patchwork fields that climbed the surrounding ridges to the eucalyptus stands and beyond to the pastures around 15,000 feet, I saw a dizzying need of arduous toil. And many fields lay idle for lack of labor. I naively assumed the problem centered on the tractor sitting useless on the side of the road like a monument more than a piece of machinery, its tires bald and flat, and the engine and transmission suffering major mechanical problems. The trouble with the tractor, though, came not from its opening up furrows in the earth, but how it cut a route for funds to cascade out of the village and into the much wealthier urban areas. The tractor sat as a monument to village exploitation.

Damian, the village broker for several concurrent development projects had located the tractor while he was in Lima. According to Damian, as villagers harassed him about the funds they had invested in him for these other projects, he produced the tractor as a gesture demonstrating that he was indeed working on behalf of the village "so people don't say bad things about me." But there was a catch. The community had to pay for registration fees and transport. Don Miguel explained that they dedicated the community crops to the tractor and that everybody additionally gave out of their pockets. Before the tractor finally arrived, they had to pay on several occasions due to unforeseen costs.

It turned out, however, that this tractor was one of 520 donated by the Japanese government and should not have cost the village anything. Further, unbeknownst to villagers, when Damian returned he took out a US$1350 loan—equivalent to roughly four annual family incomes—in the name of the community using the tractor as collateral. The village still toils under this debt. Thus, even though the tractor was supposedly free, the villagers paid for it twice. People have money they want to use to fix the tractor, but they dare not, knowing that several different parties would attempt to seize the machine.

The tractor was one of many such Trojan gifts. Cracked reservoirs, ruptured irrigation canals, and non-functional buildings dotted the community. But the tractor was worse than any of these precisely because it worked whereas most of the other projects never fully functioned. As I elaborate below, villagers had already invested almost all of their wealth with Damian, well beyond the value of several tractors. As a good faith gesture, then, the tractor proved particularly potent, getting people to keep providing Damian with money despite lacking returns on the vast sums already entrusted. Indeed, the tractor stood for the watershed moment when Damian learned that he could openly ask for ever-rising amounts of funds from the villagers, and keep them paying as long as he provided some tokenistic product. As his sister explained:

> First he made us give money for the tractor saying, and he told us: "sell your little pigs, your chickens so the tractor can arrive." Then also for acquiring the loan from the [Agrarian] Bank he said: "sell your animals, your pigs and chickens in order to pay for the procedure [*gestión*], with this we will do the procedure." After he told us that "we are going to Lima to do the procedure," and after he never returned.

Damian applied the paradigm of the tractor to many projects: leverage a flow of village funds by providing only notional returns. And villagers kept giving until Damian "stripped all the community members of their money" and disappeared.

EXPLOITATIVE DEVELOPMENT

This small story tells of a much larger dynamic. In Huaytabamba, villagers regularly decried that "the local government has always embezzled [community] funds, without really showing anything for it." Indeed, even most of the individuals who dominated these offices believed people (themselves excluded) only served for their own personal gain, insinuating some kind of overt corruption. Presidents and their cronies regularly profited from acquiring or selling off village resources, such as communal lands and stands of eucalyptus trees. Additionally, as in most of the countryside, unfinished infrastructure projects littered the community, testifying to village leader kickbacks, and inspiring villagers to condemn projects as initiated "only for stealing money." Yet despite this dissatisfaction, one coterie of villagers continually dominated the community, openly profiting from their high positions. And the majority of villagers continued to participate in these broker-led projects.

Brokers were generally villagers who came from privileged positions, having gained favor from the former hacendados by serving the central jobs of *yanacuna, caporal,* or having tight fictive kin relations. Many further differentiated themselves through using their privileges to acquire urban experiences, including education and employment, and an overall apprenticeship in the dominant culture.

Damian's biography helps explain how unique life experiences translate into privileged urban ties. Early in his life, Damian became the baptismal godson of the childless daughter of the owner of the hacienda that later became the community. Villagers generally concur with his story that she informally adopted him, taking him to the jungle town of San Francisco where she had a teaching appointment. There she provided him with a formal education, generally unheard of for villagers his age and a giant step from his illiterate father and uncles.

Close ties to this woman and the hacienda family in general helped uniquely socialize him into mestizo ways, granting him great facility with the workings of urban institutions. He claims that in 1968, at age ten, he was the most qualified to help the district judge demarcate the lands the hacendado was selling to the peasants in fear of the brewing land reform. He further claims he successfully garnered lopsided rulings for his father and other favored family members. While his closest family members dismiss his claims of degrees from the university in Ayacucho and a local technical school, the tight relationship with his privileged godmother granted him unmatched technical and cultural skills for catering to mestizo racial etiquette.

Given sufficient will (for which his socialization arguably primed him), he was uniquely positioned to create lasting and lucrative relations with urban officials—some of whom emanated from his godmother's family. And villagers readily acknowledged the esoteric skill set uniquely possessed by brokers which allowed them to access urban institutions, regularly saying these men "know how to enter the institutions," or "know how to talk to the engineers," or that they have a godfather in an agency that enables them unique privileges. Indeed, in both a mocking and self-deprecating way, villagers called Damian "Inge," short for *ingeniero* (engineer), a widely used term of endearment for any extension agent who came to the village. By this name, they mocked him for behaving like an urban functionary though he lacked credentials and a position. But they also mocked themselves for the support they invariably gave him.

In understanding the core processes driving these outcomes, researchers have frequently rejected racial analyses because phenotype plays little role, as indicated here by the fact that mestizo brokers and indigenous community members can belong to the same family (van den Berghe and Primov 1977; Albó 1994, 194; Wade 1997). As I will show, though, the intense rural-urban division and racialization of state resources means that native Quechua speakers with superior urban experiences can re-create themselves as mestizo in order to gain tremendous power in the village. In addition to distinguishing themselves through local privileges, however, brokers were the individuals who were also willing and able to prove their mestizo qualities by, among other things, assenting to do the bidding of urban functionaries interested in enlarging their networks of patronage (many of whom were former hacendados). That is, demonstrating a willingness to exploit fellow villagers proved a strong mestizo credential. A series of events in Huaytabamba demonstrates the dynamics at play.

In the mid-1980s, the former hacendado of what had become Huaytabamba told village brokers that the community actually owned almost two hundred hectares of land that the neighboring village currently controlled and had historically worked. The brokers repeatedly got villagers to donate moneys to work towards this potential windfall. The brokers sued for the territory, winning a judgment but never acquiring the land because of the other village's unwillingness to accede. In one episode, Huaytabamba paid the police to enforce the court order; but the gendarmes quickly quit the field in the face of rock-wielding opponents, leaving the Huaytabamba villagers alone to retreat bruised, without the land, and poorer.

While unsuccessful in its end goal, this experience taught village intermediaries that they could wield tremendous influence over community funds and actions, with their demonstration of urban knowledge and large promises generating unquestioned contributions even when no product was delivered. And urban institutions proved incredibly eager to leave rural governance in broker hands. To use Mahmood Mamdani's (1996) term, the brokers came to fully realize that the village was not governed by modern law but by traditional law which the brokers themselves could dictate with near impunity—at least within their own village.

At this time, central authorities and the reigning political party, Acción Popular, sought political loyalty through farming out infrastructural projects (Klarén 2000). So the village intermediaries brokered many state-sponsored programs, delivering on some projects but leaving many unfinished—and profiting on them all. These relations were enhanced through a partnership with an official of the government development agency SierraCentroSur who directed more programs towards the community seeing that the brokers were willing and able to siphon most of these funds back into the partnership. In a larger plan in the late 1980s, brokers acquired sizable low-interest loans for villagers from the new Agrarian Bank, but took half of the moneys for themselves, erroneously claiming the need to pay fees. Today, some brokers still make labyrinthine arguments that villagers owe them back payments, even though the state condemned these loans long ago. As one man described the period:

> at this time there was a lot of misappropriation of funds, as much from the community [coffers] as the public works. . . . At that time the community was used by the solicitors of works and the authorities who extracted money through faenas [communal work parties].

In addition to having villagers pay for two additional lawsuits about the contested farmlands, brokers entangled these convoluted long-term projects with a third Cattle Reactivation project which promised to upgrade and triple villagers' cattle holdings—by selling the cattle acquired through the earlier loans. One unwitting participant explained that in the mid-1990s, Damian, the lead broker

> had gathered the entire community one Saturday and they had told them that the [Cattle] Reactivation had already come out and that it is going to get here the day after tomorrow. The only thing still pending was some money to give the engineers their part. He convinced the people and told them that each person would get four bulls and money according to the quantity of money they gave. This is why they sold their horses, cows, pigs, everything in order to supply money and have [the project] finally come out. The next day which was a Sunday [the day of the livestock market] they took all their animals to the market to sell. All of this money, up through right now, has not appeared.

Villagers entrusted the majority of their capital to Damian so he could use his urban knowledge, including bribing engineers, to gain resources for the village. According to a wide variety of villagers, however, he just "put the money in his pocket; he stole the money" and disappeared. Thus, even though brokers openly profited from the projects they accessed, most of which never provided the promised services, villagers continued to follow brokers' mandates and provide them with funds. In other words, the brokerage system continued to subjugate the indigenous population, only now it occurred through the guise of developmentalist betterment.

THE DEVELOPMENTALIST INDIAN QUESTION

After the Agrarian Reform, the Indian Question evolved to address the issue of how to subjugate indigenous populations through incorporating their specific and general demands for improved wellbeing. And in this, the widespread acceptance of developmentalist ideology proved a powerful tool.

The real issue that precipitated the 1969 Agrarian Reform—and arguably those before it—was the threat of localized peasant uprisings adhering into a national movement addressing the larger inequities for which local landlord abuses were but a symptom. Among other things, Velasco's populism that promised "Peasants, the land owner [patrón] will never again feed from your poverty!" refocused attention from the national system to the local landlord. In hewing to the class identity of the rural, he predicated this limited enfranchisement not only on the indigenous having to forswear their patrimonial rights, but on rendering issues of rural poverty no longer political but technical. Now the military-populist state, supposedly in peasants' best interests, could impose development projects as solutions that just needed finer adjustments, even as it depended on the former landowners for implementation.

Further, the legislation narrowed discontent to the smallest and arguably most fraught geographic area: the village. Only in these highly insular and institutionally segregated locales could peasants exercise any kind of autonomy. Again, the government provided no budget to these entities, instead forcing them to eke out any living from paternalistic development programs and the land, limited severely by cheap food policies. Peasants become politically isolated in ineffectual institutions.

Moreover, villages inherited a legacy of conflict that they were ill equipped to confront. The Agrarian Reform stands as the greatest historical investment in standardizing land titles. But it confronted a byzantine tangle of overlapping land claims generated over centuries. First, informality has always reigned in land ownership, land parcels an important piece of patronage, but also an important resource in trade, lending, and inheritance. Moreover, since the time of the encomiendas, each successive land regime has merely placed their new system on top of the old without abrogating it. And Independence saw a proliferation of titling schemes as hacendados grabbed for land to undermine competition from peasants. Thus, lands can have multiple legitimate claims on them with no clear way to delineate ownership. As lands serve the core of people's survival strategies and identities, such confusion only furthers bloody conflicts. In the end, the Agrarian Reform relented on fixing the problem and muddied it more by adding additional forms of titling on the already muddled system.

Indeed, in Huaytabamba itself before the Reform, the hacendado made up his own titling system so he could sell his lands to the peasant

residents and not risk future confiscation. The patrón sensed major reform in the political air. He told his caporal, his local enforcer, to gather
enough families together to generate sufficient funds to buy the hacienda
piecemeal. After squeezing their social networks, they finally gathered
enough resources for an initial purchase in 1964. This largely entailed the
caporal deciding the field disbursements himself, based on contributions
and favoritism, and simply marking these in a book. This tome had no
legal standing or precedent and was never filed as a binding legal document. Instead, it simply represented a homegrown method for showing
what people reluctantly agreed to in order to acquire small parcels of
land, something almost impossible in the early 1960s. The hacendado
himself, like most of his peers during the Reform, moved on to acquire an
important position in the Agrarian Reform office itself. Thus he still controlled lands though no longer owned any. And he became a pivotal
official in the doling out of state patronage.

Indeed, while the haciendas may have been considerably dismantled,
the patróns lived on as government officials and/or monopolists of key
resources such as trucking or credit. Accessing necessary resources still
required going through these power brokers. All told, the Velasco reforms took the peasant-based discontent of the 1950s and 1960s and chan-
neled it into the land conflicts within and between villages, initially as a
technical problem of redistribution but devolving rapidly into opportunistic demonstrations of gamonal-like power, gaming the dysfunctional
system.

Racially, then, the reforms broke the back of a potentially national
pan-ethnic Indian mobilization by incorporating native demands for betterment. The turn to developmentalism obscured the racial content of
these demands by rendering them technical and about a very narrow
kind of productivity. It thereby ushered in a color-blind form of domination by making mestizos the logical developmentalist authority due to
their superior technical knowledge—by hiding the cultural and political
workings of the system as supposedly isolated technical issues.

EXCLUSION THROUGH DEVELOPMENTALIST INCLUSION

The developmentalist structure inherited the key facets of its historical
antecedents, though has altered and revitalized them in important ways.
The principal end goal entails central authorities achieving native acquiescence. But this is an indirect outcome achieved through proxies. The
crucial relations achieving this objective occur around the position of
mestizo broker, and are therefore the central focus here. These relations
push brokers to exploit and rule despotically over their indigenous
wards, amounting to a revitalized form of indirect rule I call "authoritarian intermediation." The normal structures and practices of the institu-

tions linking villages to the city concentrate all local power into the broker position, predicating this privileged position upon fulfilling urban
priorities of a tractable rural clientele. And complex, fluid, and historically emergent cultural understandings ensure that only a select few individuals who can most convincingly demonstrate their mestizo credentials will operate as brokers. In all, the institutional forms and cultural
practices combine to make the rural-urban link as narrow as possible,
thereby vesting all local power in the few individuals who can bridge this
divide, and predicating their privileged position on continuing the historic flow of native resources into urban power centers.

More specifically, the system creates a self-reinforcing Exploitation-
Authoritarian Cycle (figure 3.1) in which greater broker success causes
their native wards to become increasingly politically dependent and economically exploited. Natives must access external resources through the
few local individuals who are willing and able to act according to mestizo
urban cultural norms. As indicated in figure 3.1, however, accessing urban projects entails providing urban functionaries with rural resources,
itself a display of mestizo cultural wherewithal. This tribute endears brokers to urban patrons, enhancing the personalistic relationships through
which patronage networks distribute funds. As broker-functionary relations build, programs can grow in complexity and duration. Spearheading larger and multiple projects enhances broker authority in the village,
increasing their local impunity and legitimacy.

The larger and more involved a program, the more funds brokers can
take from villagers, and the more they can keep delaying the eventual
payoff. As program acquisition requires community subsidization, intertwining simultaneous programs helps obscure the source, destiny, and
eventual results of funds, increasing villager dependence as resources

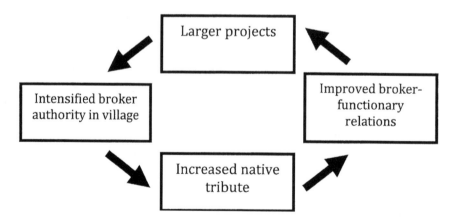

Figure 3.1.   The Exploitation-Authoritarian Cycle

increasingly circulate out of their hands. Like an authoritarian Ponzi scheme dictating that "investors" never withdraw their money but keep it cycling within the system, brokers can gain control over tremendous sums—relative to the impoverished Peruvian highlands—over which they enjoy ever-increasing impunity. Villagers, meanwhile, become increasingly dependent on and exercise less restraint over the brokers. Villager options consist of acquiescing to demands for more contributions in the hopes of recovering what they have already given, or withdrawing with the consequences of writing off their losses and shearing their connections to the urban core. These relations can spiral to fantastic levels of peculation after which withdrawal becomes the majority decision; but this breaking point has proven dramatically high. The following sections detail the workings of this system and how it particularly played out in Huaytabamba.

INSTITUTIONAL RACIALIZATION

To alleviate indigenous poverty levels, the World Bank (2005) suggests increasing education and health funding. The new social service programs of the 1990s, however, respectively spent 50 percent and 25 percent of their $141 million annual expenditures on precisely these two items, and poverty rates actually increased (Gonzales de Olarte 1998, 62). *Pace* the World Bank, I found that indigenous marginalization in highland Peru is not so much the result of being left out as the particular way natives are incorporated.

Highland communities predominantly access the urban power center through what is called the solicitor [*gestor*] system. This distinctly native system links the village institutions to urban organizations, forming the backbone of racialized indirect rule. Solicitors gain all power over the resources they broker, predicated upon using these to further endear themselves into urban patronage networks. As such, rather than fulfilling rural needs, the system bolsters urban patronage networks through maintaining a compliant rural clientele. This governing structure descends from the notoriously corrupt and rapacious colonial town councils, cabildos (a term still sometimes used in villages), through which Europeans concentrated all local power in order to dominate the native populations (Klarén 2000).

The fuel for the solicitor system originates in state or international organizations making resources available for rural areas. Funds pass to agents in the relevant highland cities—in this case Ayacucho—who generally either work as poorly paid functionaries in government institutions like the Ministry of Agriculture, or for an internationally funded non-governmental organizations (NGOs) like CARE, World Vision, or ADRA (Adventist Development and Relief Agency). To pass through the native color line and reach rural villages, these resources must engage the main engine of the solicitor system, therein institutionally segregating highland villages by making them governed through the distinctly "native" yet authoritarian system inherent to indirect rule.

Urban service programs work with a single village representative in whom they vest all local control. When ADRA was planning its latest projects, for instance, the organization's official only negotiated with one man. This man Antonio, the son of the Evangelical church founder don Alfonso, also served as an Evangelical pastor and had regularly occupied the office of president and sub-mayor. He later moved to the city and stopped practicing the new religion. However, with the ADRA official he met in a small dimly lit room, the two quietly decided how to spend the organization's money and how the villagers would contribute their labor to the program. In a much larger example, the Agrarian Bank, above, entrusted all village loans to a single individual who lacked collateral and accountability, resulting in this man taking over half the funds and the government writing off most of the loans as it did across the country.

In sync with urban institutions, villagers expect that only one of their members will seek, locate, arrange, and administer resources from the city. The solicitor system is engrained in village political practices through the regularly elected community president whose chief role is to solicit projects for the village. This is the ethnic heart of the village, with community membership assuming compliance to the presidents and their projects. Similarly, the only accountability over the president consists of ethnically based calls to safeguard villagers "like his children," and a *fiscal* or prosecutor elected as part of the governing junta who has never fulfilled the office obligations of filing charges for presidential malfeasance. Fiscals lack motivation to fulfill office responsibilities as they are elected in concert—rather than in conflict—with their presidents. Herein the corrupt legacy of the cabildo makes itself highly visible, the only oversight actually functioning to help concentrate presidential power.

The institutions of the solicitor system, then, establish a framework in which single village representatives exercise exclusive power over the resources they broker, personifying the extremely narrow bottleneck linking the village to the city. The same few individuals regularly served in this role, wearing many hats, and dominating every program. While these are generally the most experienced and successful villagers, marking them in some way as natural leaders, their domination has more to do with their personalistic relationships to urban power holders and their ability to cater to the demands of the clientelistic means of service delivery.

Just as local ethnic ideologies help provide unquestioning support to solicitors, they also bolster the system's extreme clientelism that makes rural-urban relations particularly exploitative. In particular, the current ethnic construction of community government equates autonomy with lacking any direct institutional connections. These echo the anti-exploitation Agrarian Reform rhetoric, but generally reflect elite assertions to determine local policy. Practically speaking, though, this means that community presidents are not plugged in to a larger political infrastructure which confers entitlements based on need, merit, or coherent policy goals.

While governments at other levels (department, province, and municipality) enjoy specific budgets tied to the federal government, no parallel exists for community government. Instead, presidents must go hat in hand to urban offices to beg resources, making native resource delivery highly personalistic and paternalistic in character.[2] Local ethnic constructions of community autonomy buoy this structural isolation, equating formal institutional connections with outside interference. At the same time, though, villagers widely recognize that they must establish clientelistic relations with urban power holders in order to acquire external resources. As such, villagers are frequently prepared to pay various subsidies, such as dedicating crops to urban functionaries, offering free labor, supporting political candidates, or simply providing money in order to get in their good graces.

As one man described his village's relation with an urban official: "we took photos together, we thanked him by slaughtering pigs. We received him by smothering him with all kinds of attention; when he complied with his word we gave him this affection." In other words, while the urban official was simply doing his job of delivering programs to rural communities, the villagers knew they had to reciprocate with an outsized response in hopes of acquiring future projects. Corruption is pervasive in Peru, with surveys showing that the population overwhelmingly believes it is heavily entrenched and "that impunity is the rule in Peru, not the exception" (Rotta and Narvarte Olivares 2006, 224; Transparency International 2006). The reliance on personalistic ties in an atmosphere of overt corruption sets up a dynamic in which villagers and city functionaries expect that kickbacks are a regular facet of service delivery. Urban power holders will not deliver unless they get something in return.

Other institutional facets of the community further enable the extraction of subsidies. The solicitor model in and of itself requires villagers to make contributions towards program acquisition, as demonstrated above by people willingly selling their animals to provide kickbacks to the urban engineers. Further, the faena system of communal work parties poises villagers to launch immediately into the physical labor requirements of the programs, including the work necessary to maintain personalistic networks, such as painting patrons' houses or dedicating an entire crop to them. Most faenas are totally unfunded projects functioning economically as a tax on locals to help maintain their village infrastructure. The faena system emerges from a strong and diffuse local ethnic ideology of community much more widely shared and incorporated into life strategies than the more elite ideology of autonomy, one man explaining to me that "without faena we are nothing, we are not a community."

The injection of external resources into this work system relieves individual burdens acquired through faena mandates, predisposing villagers to embrace whatever funds enter the system and make their labor available to the given project. External projects thereby become easily and quickly incorporated into the community system. Village elite can frequently buy themselves out of community labor responsibilities or simply work as project administrators, further distinguishing themselves from the masses (cf. Gose 1994). So primed are all the other villagers by this system, however, they are generally at a loss to explain their participation in any complex way, instead seeing it simply as normal: "when there is something, we are all there," one man explained to me. The ethnically bound faena system thereby tends to reinforce local ethnic identification. At the same time, however, it presents brokers and other urban officials with a ready and tractable labor force generally eager to fulfill even overtly corrupt schemes. The ethnically generated workforce, then, provides the means to enact strategies emanating from the mestizo urban center, that is, to fulfill a highly racialized agenda.

The villagers have little recourse against such exploitation. Even with few results, people continually gave to the above projects. While the leading broker, in his direct partnership with an urban functionary, extolled grand promises and complex explanations of future windfalls, the money was forever circling out of the villagers' hands, justified partially by the delivery of small amounts of programs from which the brokers profited disproportionately. As recounted by this broker's brother (indicating that family provides little insulation from exploitation):

> The people trusted now that they did not want to lose the money they had given previously. So we were going to recover our money if the engineer was here [working on small projects]. We were also very worried because we had entrusted him with the money without signing a document.

Having already invested beyond their means into the various projects, the villagers found that the only way they could try to recover their money was to keep working with and giving money to the urban functionary. Villagers felt they had no recourse but to utilize local ethnic social norms, making the agent an extended member of their community. City institutions provided no remedy. Villagers lacked the requisite urban mestizo norms—embodied here by a signed document. Instead, they had to try and tie the functionary to the community, increasing his ethnic obligations by providing more contributions. The racial divide between town and country, then, not only isolates natives into weak ethnic enclaves, it enables a feedback loop in which functionaries can fulfill their urban mestizo priorities by increasing community ethnic exploitation.

In this way, urban officials look to use their control over resources to extend their networks of patronage. For instance, a man running for district mayor promised funds for a new school (through a local intermediary) in exchange for villager support in the election. However, the new mayor's proffered school, built by donated village labor, has always remained flooded with stagnant water and has never provided any educational benefit (see chapter 4). Similarly, regardless of intention, the structure of the Agrarian Bank lending program funneled resources to the locally powerful, resulting in solidifying the traditional authoritarian means of political control rather than increasing popular economic productivity. The political-value of programs in their ability to extend patronage networks far outstrips their use-value in serving the population, such as schools providing education or canals providing water, generally increasing mestizo power while undermining natives' positions.

Overall, with urban and community institutions vesting all power in single individuals, the solicitor system creates the position of local despot to represent indigenous villages. This position must be exclusive and exploitative as the system's clientelism ensures that only the few villagers who create strong connections with urban patronage networks through providing a tractable rural clientele can represent the village. These findings echo the insights of the racial analyses of the 1970s, with racialization caused by a particular form of political economic integration. Specifically:

> (1) natives are subjugated as subjects: natives lack citizen rights; they must depend for personhood upon their local despotic patrons whose own citizenship depends on the continued disenfranchisement of their clients; and
> (2) natives are subjugated as natives: the normal workings of the current system reproduce the colonial system of indirect rule.

At the local level, ethnicity enables this racial domination by

> (1) helping to preclude the village from non-arbitrary institutionalized connections to the larger society, and
> (2) helping to marshal local resources with which to shore up the clientelist mestizo system.

Unlike the structural analyses of the 1970s that saw culture as unchanging, however, my work indicates that the fluidity of culture, particularly the ability of groups to alter culture so as to keep it esoteric and exclusionary, plays important roles in maintaining the system of indirect rule, a point I turn to now.

CULTURAL RACIALIZATION

Ever-shifting cultural practices enable brokers to make their exclusive connections to urban patronage networks. Even though a wide variety of factors contribute to peoples' racial classification in Latin America, a broad spectrum of scholars and most of the populace agree that race in Peru, as well as in much of Latin America, generally follows a tripartite hierarchical division, running from whites through mestizos, and down to natives at the bottom (Vargas Llosa 1990; de la Cadena 2000; Hale 2006). Whereas the works on cultural politics emphasize cultural malleability as creating new means of inclusion, in the case of highland Peru culture enables vibrant means of exclusion wherein dominant groups can continuously change the rules of the game to safeguard their privileges.

Tapping into the historically constituted power of mestizaje requires successfully employing multiple aspects of mestizo cultural capital (Bourdieu 1986). Acquiring and maintaining the position of mestizo *broker* requires employing the further cultural capital specific to urban institutions, or operating according to their mestizo racial etiquette: the "set of interpretive codes and racial meanings which operate in the interactions of daily life" which confer status and hierarchy in the social system (Omi and Winant 1994, 60). A major aspect of this etiquette entails bolstering urban networks with rural resources. Once brokers deliver, they acquire a relationship with an urban functionary who will then more willingly provide further projects. In this way, brokers achieve the unique resource of institutional approval, the most valuable form of cultural capital. With such capital, brokers can increase their stocks through their more authoritative village control over ever-larger urban originating programs.

To be successful, however, brokers must regularly assert their mestizo credentials at both the community and urban levels, thereby continuously retracing the color line and continuing the state mestizaje project of denigrating the Indian. Only through such regular assertions do they stave off the risk of suffering a similar racialization as the majority of villagers, and do they garner the wages of racial privilege. This is a highly racialized process of cultural distinction as it (1) furthers the construction of natives as anti-modern, (2) predicates mestizo inclusion on continued native subjugation, and (3) vitalizes the cycle of increased native villager exploitation and enhanced mestizo broker authority.

Cultural capital exists in three forms: embodied, objectified, and institutionalized (Bourdieu 1986). The embodied state largely refers to acquired cultural knowledge, most obviously manifesting itself in Peru through the use of language. Mestizos not only display Spanish fluency and non-Andean accents, but a ready familiarity with a variety of cultural references. As Quechua, spoken by the majority of highland residents, lacks any consistent didactic materials or even a unified spelling scheme, the distinguishing power of language cannot be overstated. And further embodied distinctions in comportment, behavior, pastimes, music, festivals, religious practices, education, and employment permeate the Andes. Objectified cultural capital encompasses material objects and is more readily apparent, with indigenous people tending to wear broad-brimmed hats and sandals, while people can distinguish themselves as mestizo through closed-toed shoes, pressed Western clothing, and the full accoutrement of urban living (van den Berghe and Primov 1977; Weismantel 1988; Portocarrero 1993; Lagos 1994; Degregori 1995; de la Cadena 2000; Yezer 2008). Where most anyone could use their economic capital to quickly acquire the objectified form, only with sufficient embodied cultural capital can people consume these goods in a culturally appropriate way.

Institutionalized cultural capital, however, in its capacity to confer status upon agents, proves the most determinant in the Andean relations of rule. While objectified and embodied capital help brokers gain institutional recognition, enjoying the endorsement of mestizo urban networks bestows tremendous village-level power upon brokers. Indeed, such coveted cultural resources enable the concentration of village power in a single person, enabling them to speak and act in its name.[3] That is, these high concentrations of *cultural* capital enable brokers to embody the village's *social* capital—its ability to put people into action.

Mestizo brokers display all forms of cultural capital at the frequent meetings held in the villages, making these much more sites of racial domination than expressions of "a community's collective vision of its goals" (Warren and Jackson 2003, 29; cf. Petras and Morley 1992). Mestizo brokers do not attend most village meetings as the focus tends to be too parochial; for example the Mothers' Club sponsored weekly cleaning of the central square. As one exception, a broker representing the district mayor once charged into a Mothers' Club meeting in a pickup truck—any vehicle a rare visitor—loaded with federally funded foodstuffs which he quickly distributed to new mothers. This man therein presented himself as the village's own outsider, above the tedium of regular meetings, but magnanimously using his wherewithal for the good of the village. While the mothers would have received these goods regardless, by grafting his identity onto this mestizo program he validates the authoritarian idea that the few people like him, by knowing the mestizo city and the native village, can best decide and deliver what is best for the community, while actually doing nothing at all.

Rather than providing enlightened leadership, though, brokers do more to obfuscate the mestizo urban core, making it seem impenetrable and thereby making themselves appear invaluable to the village. The few meetings they do attend are central to community affairs. Sometimes brokers make great displays of condescending to come to the meetings which take away from their more crucial affairs in the city. One man once arrived over the gouged roads in a taxi, therein displaying a time-poor but money-rich image which dramatically contrasts villagers' long walks to their small fields.

When brokers attend, they dominate. As discussed above, mestizo brokers tend to hold the most important local offices because of their privileged connections to the city. But even when they have no official authority, they assume central roles at meetings and do most of the talking. Their self-presentation exudes mestizo objectified cultural capital: tight haircuts, fancy watches, and trim clothes while eschewing the broad-brimmed hats, patched clothes, and retread tire sandals of the majority. This starkly demarcates mestizos as "better," as able to function in the outside world in a matter-of-fact way alien to villagers, thereby vesting local mestizos with seemingly inherent authority. And their actions at these meetings also work to exacerbate native alienation from the urban core. Rather than trying to effect understanding, brokers usually launch into long-winded descriptions of urban processes and projects, generating confusion rather than enlightenment.

These political-cultural distinctions also show themselves in comportment. At meetings, for instance, most villagers engage in a high context manner, acknowledging the importance of social connections through thanking a list of people before they make a statement. In contrast, mestizo brokers and urban agents tend to skip these aspects and immediately speak on specific issues. Similarly, villagers generally engage with urban functionaries through a paternalist dialogue, villager obsequiousness matched by urban condescension, including a pervasive use of childish names like "my little son" or "little father." This alone reinforces the cultural gap, insisting that these individuals will never engage openly, but only as people on different levels of the hierarchy. In contrast, brokers tend to engage in easy fraternal dialogue with functionaries, alienating villagers by overtly displaying an affinity unavailable to them.

INSTITUTIONALIZED CULTURAL CAPITAL

While community meetings provide a local venue for distinction and domination, the authoritarian racialization of resources primarily emanates from urban institutions themselves. Acquiring the power of institutionalized cultural capital generally requires entering into a reciprocal relationship with an urban functionary. Once such a relationship is demonstrated, particularly through the delivery of projects and resources, institutionalized cultural capital makes brokers increasingly unassailable in their local positions, enabling greater impunity over larger village sums.

The racial etiquette of these institutions creates enormous cultural barriers to entry, with the result of screening out the majority and selecting a small minority. To illustrate this, I contrast the interactions I had with one urban institution to the relationship a village broker developed with another. While my attempts to create an institutional link with CARE-Peru only resulted in humiliation for myself and the non-broker villager with whom I worked, the relationship between a village broker and another functionary blossomed to the point of establishing their own organization, DICCPUM, through which they were able to dramatically increase villager exploitation and spread their "services" to other geographic areas.

A villager and I approached the local office of CARE-Peru to solicit funds ($400) for the cement and roofing materials of a compost producing facility that the villager had designed. I naively believed that the villager provided sufficient authenticity to show this was a productive grassroots project, and that I brought professionalism in the form of a clearly articulated plan, including a printed proposal with a timetable and budget, detailed drawings, and a compost committee notarized book of minutes.

Two major results emerged from our meeting. First, my village colleague did not want to enter the CARE building. While it was an imposing structure reflecting foreign wealth and power, only when we entered and the CARE functionary began systematically humiliating my compatriot did I understand his reluctance. The CARE official treated the villager like a misbehaving child, dismissing his ideas, knowledge, and presence as utterly trivial. The other result was that the official extracted a tribute from me in the form of my "volunteering" for another of his projects on the promise of engaging our plan in the future—which he never did. No one ever met me when I volunteered, turning my efforts into a wasted, uncomfortable day-long trip and another humiliation; but it enhanced the agent's prestige within his network by showing he could manipulate a gringo (an inescapably marked category of wealth and power) to serve his whims.

Humiliating the villager was clearly a regular practice, displaying power but also serving as a test and a potential rite of passage. Racism, however, provided its base, with the official denigrating the villager and all he represented as irredeemable. While both the villager and I hoped to get in his good graces by acting obsequiously, in retrospect, the agent employed a highly culturally bound way to seek reciprocity for entrée into his extended network. I felt we asked for a fairly trivial sum that promised an easily reproducible way to enhance the productivity of the poorest of the poor (an aspect of CARE's mission). My meritocratic gringo proposal found no purchase, nor did the villager's local knowledge. Instead, we were supposed to offer a meaningful way to enhance this agent's network, part of which entailed proving we could force him to fulfill his promise.

Under horrible conditions, the villager was supposed to prove he was not a degraded Indian but someone who could speak the manager's own cultural language and deliver for the network by maintaining a regular but uneven reciprocal relationship. While I faced no mortifying cultural test, I would have had to have entered into a relation in which my continual work for the agent would force his compliance. As with the police running from the field in the Huaytabamba land dispute, enforcement mechanisms mostly remain informal and are based on an understanding about the inherent superiority of mestizo urban culture and the undeservingness of rural highland society. Not only did we lack the right cultural knowledge and economic leverage to access resources, we quickly became contemptible and easily exploited subjects.

Admittedly, CARE must screen their supplicants so their handouts will not get siphoned away and support competing patronage networks. For instance, as villagers became more desperate and lacking any control over Cattle Reactivation, they acquired a soil conservation project from a different service provider. These funds similarly disappeared after villagers sent them to the Reactivation broker and functionary in Lima who said they "just lacked a few signatures" and needed money for the final processing [*gestionando*]. With the normalcy of such extortion, then, personal relationships best guarantee the proper use of funds. But these funds likewise are the best resource for solidifying such relationships, strongly reinforcing the personalism at the core of resource provision. And, as shown here, mestizo racial etiquette becomes shorthand for screening the individuals who understand these rules of the game.

In contrast to my stymied attempts to solicit CARE, the tight relationships village brokers enjoyed with their partner at SierraCentroSur, described above, demonstrate that adroit mestizo cultural competence in the urban sphere results in exploitative authoritarianism in the community. Damian in particular was uniquely positioned to develop a mutually beneficial relationship with his contact at SierraCentroSur, including a paid position for himself, as long as he continued to bring village funds back into the relationship. In the building of a village reservoir, for instance, Damian successfully siphoned funds earmarked for village labor costs. Villagers complained that the smallness of the reservoir limited its agricultural use, whereas the daily wages would have provided a welcome relief, which was most likely the populist government's main intention. Thus, providing a tangible resource helped solidify the broker-agent relations and the broker's authoritarian and exploitative local power, with these funds remaining in the hands of the broker and his urban partner.

Through skimming resources from such projects, Damian and his partner formed and financed their own agency, DICCPUM (Integrated Development for Peasant Communities and Marginal Urban Areas) through which they could launch more projects, set up operations in

Lima, and expand their geographic and exploitative scope. In particular, through DICCPUM they launched the Cattle Reactivation project. As villagers described it, "bringing us these works they were going to go to Lima, this was definitely their intention." That is, rather than focused on building village infrastructure, the functionary and Damian—this witness's brother—brought tangible if ersatz results through small project in order to establish DICCPUM in Lima. And from this less accountable position they could launch the Reactivation and eventually strip villagers of all their resources.

Damian bragged to me that he had worked throughout Ayacucho and three other departments and had various women throughout the country. As one man bitterly recalled, "He kept us dizzy with his different plans. . . . I went to Lima and I found him living in a hotel, a good hotel, eating always in restaurants . . . and from that moment we started distrusting and he disappeared and we knew we had been fooled." In all, the institutional cultural capital achieved through catering to urban mestizo demands for a compliant rural clientele created a circular and cumulative relationship wherein the funds siphoned from the community intensified broker authority and the ability to take greater resources until villagers paid astronomical amounts for a project, Reactivation, that provided no results at all.

Together, the institutional forms and the cultural practices provide the cumulative and circular causality pushing for continued native subordination. The distinctly indigenous governing apparatus militates for rural authoritarianism while culture delineates between the privileged and the exploited, the legitimate from the incompetent. Bringing rural resources to support urban patronage networks grants brokers despotic control over ever-larger programs while providing them with unmatchable institutionalized cultural capital. This enhanced authority allows for the greater extraction of village resources and a spiraling cycle that rigidifies the durable inequalities between mestizos and natives.

MAKING RACISM NORMAL

While my description of these practices of distinction may make them appear to require constant, deliberate actions, they are actually highly naturalized as part of normal day-to-day routines, making this racism both pervasive and incredibly difficult to overcome. Urban functionaries maintain their jobs by controlling limited resources. They need personal relationships to guarantee the funds will be used appropriately, while at the same time they need the funds to guarantee these relationships. Given the historical process of state mestizaje, these agents, in effect, are safeguarding their group's monopoly control over these positions, practicing what Max Weber (1968 [1922], 43) calls social closure, or, looking more at hierarchy, what Charles Tilly (1998) terms opportunity hoarding. While such practices implicitly equate to exploitation, their repeated use also reveals their culturally entrenched nature as the cheapest, default way of operating. The outward manifestation is that natives are seen as largely incapable of handling resources; but the cause lies in vested interests seeking to maintain the status quo.

Rather than going out of their way to exclude the majority, urban agents do so simply by falling back on long-standing—though ever-morphing—practices. In such, as with much racialized resource distribution throughout the world, urban officials simply need to provide the resources to the individuals they are naturally predisposed to. And because this tends to occur at a subconscious level, basing resource distribution on simple cultural affinity has been shown to powerfully perpetuate racial inequality across multiple arenas, such as job hiring in the United States (Neckerman and Kirschenman 1991; Brief et al. 1995; Pager and Quillian 2005) and in Peru (MacIsaac and Patrinos 1995). This is readily visible in rural Peru. Villagers regularly defer to the natural local leaders [*dirigentes*] and urban agents deal almost exclusively with the same group. Doing otherwise would run against commonsense.

This deep racialization of urban institutions has major self-reinforcing mechanisms in which, barring major structural changes, the brokers do represent the village's best immediate chance at acquiring external resources despite the standard practices of peculation. Brokers did bring some limited positive results through their projects. Even though villagers were supposed to receive all of the Agrarian Bank loans, they still received half, amounting to unprecedented sums. While most people sold the animals they bought with these loans in order to finance the Cattle Reactivation, successful brokers can deliver tangible results well beyond the capacity of most villagers. Similarly, while Damian ended up with all the money earmarked for labor, he did provide a reservoir, however small and prone to failure. And another broker did acquire the new primary school; the lack of accountability in the system did not have to result in it being permanently flooded.

Just as these few individual mestizos successfully bring resources to the community, however faulty, brokerage by non-mestizos—people unwilling or unable to conform to mestizo racial etiquette—generally proves fruitless. One villager, for instance, pointed to the small garden at the primary school as the apex of his presidential accomplishments. The election of such non-elites amounts more to a protest of broker corruption rather than any kind of meaningful alternative. The populace voiced two general critiques of village leadership, accusing officials of either lazy incompetence or corruption. Villagers labeled non-brokers with sloth as they failed to bring resources to the village because they lacked sufficient connections. On the other hand, villagers denounced elite brokers as corrupt and sometimes even threatened official complaints. However, the experienced brokers weathered such criticism and remained the key representatives of the community. As one NGO worker complained to me, "those who lead are not the ones who rule," meaning that brokers worked in the name of the village regardless of office title, and that the community provided little restraint over these true power holders.

And continued villager support must be understood within the context of impoverished rural Peru. Amid such scarcity, villagers welcome all projects as potential opportunities. That most projects, regardless of who brokers them, sit half-finished or in disrepair provides grist for complaints, but also shapes expectations about normal outcomes and the complications behind finishing even the simplest project. An earthquake in Pakistan prevented ADRA from delivering USAID-donated foodstuffs. CARE promised, and failed to deliver, a small roof once villagers built the adobe walls of a guinea pig farm because anti-CARE coca farmer protests in the jungle caused a complete institutional overhaul. In this environment, brokers are at least tacitly forgiven for their total failures— a half-built chapel, a treeless arboretum—while their limited successes— a leaky reservoir, faulty outhouses—appear unmatchable.

Further, exploitation, particularly in the form of unremunerated labor, is an inbuilt aspect of community life. The faena system at the heart of local ethnic identity primes villagers to provide free labor. The hope is that unpaid labor will bear future fruit. But this only happens infrequently and, perhaps ironically, mostly with broker-sponsored projects (though not with most of their projects). An ethnically bound developmentalist ideology that villagers must work for the good of the community provides the faith behind such labor donation. Brokers providing a range of projects, a few of which have some limited quality, enable them ever-greater authority up to the point of fantastic failures like Reactivation.

At this point, villagers can react severely, particularly against the institution that enabled their exploitation. After Reactivation failed, villagers "lost all faith in the [community] authorities and then came the destruction; the community become totally disorganized; they would not even give a little bit so the [new] authorities couldn't do anything." But this also helps the brokers who generally have gained tremendously through such Ponzi schemes. Instead of reforming community government to achieve some justice against rapacious intermediaries, villagers end up dismantling what amounts to their primary vehicle for ethnic mobilization. The entrenchment of community government in the structures of despotic resource procurement thereby forces villagers to choose between a government which is exploitative or ineffectual. But because the community represents the best chance to secure external resources, villagers eventually return to it. And villagers end up supporting the same brokers or their cronies as they, with their considerable institutional cultural capital, are best positioned to remobilize the community.

Finally, culturalist racist rationalizations present the unequal social relations as normal. Specifically, this ideology blames the indigenous population for its own poverty, naturalized as individual failures to compete successfully in the larger mestizo culture (cf. de la Cadena 2000). Extorting rural resources is not seen as exploitation but simply as greater competitive success. "Look, anybody can walk into the [urban] agencies," Damian regularly intoned to me, meaning that resources are available to any individual who has the courage and character to ask. Individuals who successfully access state resources are free to use them as a reward for their hard work. Others legitimately miss out on the resources because they lost a fair competition.

Village elite similarly expressed culturalist prejudicial attitudes purporting to explain the overall situation of continued inequality. A man I regarded as very thoughtful and not opportunistic explained to me that "the problem we have here is a lack of culture," elaborating this to mean that "the people will not educate themselves."[4] Many others also regularly stressed the impoverished destiny people faced by not prioritizing education but instead spending their money on their animals. More frequently, elites relied on tropes about individual characteristics, declaring that the "campesinos are not ambitious," or "are very *conformista*," or "do not put in the necessary work, and they lack knowledge and experience," or more simply they "are accustomed to handouts and get lazier." The most powerful trope, however, consisted of pointing to all the failed projects in the village which the elite were good enough to broker but which the villagers could not maintain.

In sum, with these practices deep-seated in local culture, racial inequality persists through people at all levels going about their normal business, rather than through people acting from malicious bigotry. Urban officials entrust resources to the broker with whom they share a natural empathy. Intermediaries do what a natural leader needs to do in order to safeguard future resources for the community. Villagers, facing a scarcity in which ersatz projects represent wealth, support brokers politically and with labor and funds. And culturalist racism provides the rationalizations through which mestizo "power secures its dominance by seeming not to be anything in particular" (Lipsitz 1995, quoting Dyer 1988).

CONCLUSION: THE RACIST SUCCESS OF FAILED DEVELOPMENT

Over fifteen years ago, Mary Weismantel and Stephen F. Eisenman (1998, 122) urged scholars to return racial analyses to indigenous Latin America as, among other reasons, the predominating ethnic analysis "works to remove from view the historical specificity of oppression." Since then, very little headway has been made, particularly in identifying the sources of durable racial inequalities.

In this chapter, I have articulated the primary elements of the Peruvian racialized social structure under developmentalism that militate for continued indigenous subordination. Specifically, a system of indirect rule institutionally segregates natives into ethnic enclaves ruled despotically by mestizo intermediaries whose own privileged position depends on facilitating native exploitation. The institutions linking native villages to the city facilitate local despotic rule. Predicating resource access on mestizo cultural know-how ensures that only a few villagers with mestizo priorities will ever serve this role. And the clientelistic manner of resource allocation makes the system particularly exploitative, with rural resources primarily bolstering urban patronage networks. Because it is embodied by mestizo authoritarian intermediaries, native success results in strengthening the color line, increasing the power of local despots and their ability to exploit their indigenous wards.

Empirically, this manifests itself in the two intertwining questions of how brokers have so much power and why villagers continually offer support. That these questions partially answer each other — villager backing makes brokers powerful while broker power entices villager support — helps explain the durability of racial inequalities. But power emanates from the urban core. Brokers have so much power because urban institutions need a single individual who will locally oversee projects in such a way as to invigorate their urban clientelist network. Urban agents need a personal relationship with brokers to safeguard the appropriate use of funds, and funds best fortify these relations. As brokers build their urban connections, then, their despotic ability and motivation to exploit the village only increase. But, overall, since urban officials largely do not see anything intrinsically wrong with the system, these dynamics mostly serve to keep everyone, particularly natives, in their place.

Similarly, since brokers are vested with so much urban power, they represent villagers' best chances to access resources, even with exploitation endemic. Poor infrastructure and failed projects make up the legacy of indigenous rural Peru. The rare ability to initially access scarce external resources, coupled with a few limited successes, maintains community support. Villagers readily recognize the costs and risks of project acquisition. But they are almost always eager to face these because of their impoverished situations. Rather than making cold cost-benefit analyses, villagers are instead desperately seeking external resources to make their labor productive, just as in the most traditional forms of exploitation. The system can spiral up to spectacularly extortive actions, like the Reactivation; but these are made up of the many small exploitive events through which communities acquire their few poor resources — the leaky reservoirs, dirty potable water systems, non-private privies, and collapsing potato barns. Villagers will temporarily withdraw from the community system, the closest manifestation of the engine of their exploitation; but their lack of options will slowly draw them back.

Through illustrating these relations, I have aimed to show that the regeneration of the position of authoritarian intermediary, rather than any individual broker, is responsible for perpetuating native subordination. Instead of a choice between authoritarian and non-authoritarian village representation, potential community leaders face the conundrum of local despotism or ineffectiveness, while villagers face the choice between exploitative or inept leadership. Even when natives have come to occupy this position, as Charles R. Hale (2004) shows for Guatemala, they are forced to make hard choices between becoming an "authorized Indian" revitalizing the racist system by giving it a native face or being cast as self-marginalizing and even terrorists. The position matters much more than who occupies it. And in the case of Huaytabamba, Damian's schemes cycled up to such high levels of extraction that once he finally disappeared, he left villagers economically bereft and politically unwilling to participate in even the most trusted parts of local governance, with little sign as to how the village could recover.

NOTES

1. This chapter is a revised version of Scarritt (2011).

2. Mainstream analyses of patronage in governments across the globe (for example, "Earmarks" in the United States) explain that competition between patronage sources forestall the excesses witnessed in earlier eras of machine politics, a restraint the highland solicitor system mostly lacks (Roniger and Güneş-Ayata 1994).

3. Or as Bourdieu puts it: "institutionalized forms of delegation which enable [the village] to concentrate the totality of social capital . . . in the hands of a single agent or a small group of agents and to mandate this plenipotentiary, charged with *plena potestas agendi et loquendi* [full power to act and speak], to represent the group, to speak and act in its name" (1986, 251).

4. In Spanish, "cultura" can translate directly to "culture" or mean something closer to "education," as the speaker intends it here. But such an understanding of education entails significant assimilationist aspects, continuing the notion that villagers are to blame for their own situation because they do not want to "better" themselves by conforming to the urban mestizo culture.

FOUR

Evangelical Ethnic Revitalization

While Damian worked his extortive machinations,[1] some villagers began converting to Evangelical Protestantism.[2] During one of their first meetings:

> There was a bush behind the [meeting] house where they placed dynamite and detonated it; my cousin Hilario [a later convert] and other people did this; I wanted to go out and see and they told me "don't go out, if they're the terrorists they will leave us papers"; when we went to see in the morning they had left a paper where they told us to quit being Evangelists.

In other words, converts faced vehement hostility. Catholics saw Protestant conversion as a direct threat to their lifestyle and wellbeing. The almost nightly cacophony of overlapping, keening pleas directly to God deeply offended Catholic sensibilities, especially its masculinist aspects like emotional restraint. And new behavioral mores threatened the village as an institution, with community-wide activities tied tightly to the Catholic calendar of events involving Evangelically forbidden high alcohol consumption and dancing.

One current Evangelical stalwart admitted that "back then I did not like the Evangelicals, I hated them; I told the others to take them and kick the Evangelicals out of this village." Malicious rumors spread: "the people who are now Evangelical told us [early Evangelicals] that we slept around," a rumor that persists in some Catholic circles today, one man claiming that "the Evangelicals are womanizers," and that an Evangelical man in another town proselytized by offering up his daughters for sexual liaisons. In all, a violent splintering marked Evangelism's beginning in Huaytabamba, a characteristic many other researchers have found regarding Protestant conversion in Latin America.

But by the time Damian disappeared in 1994, he had caused much more damage, leaving Huaytabamba impoverished and dysfunctional. Beyond losing most of their resources, these experiences made villagers unwilling to participate in their most vital and long-standing community organizations. Trust evaporated and villagers viewed local political offices as inherently fraudulent and exploitative.

By 1998, however, the community had totally revived itself. And the new Evangelical Protestantism largely enabled this to happen. The burgeoning churches had remained largely untouched by Damian's schemes. This was due to several factors, similar to those found in other Evangelical experiences. At this time, the congregation was largely inwardly focused on being good Christians. With the church, people sought calmness and positive socializing with likeminded Evangelicals. And believers went there specifically to shed the worries of their secular lives. In other words, at this point, the politics of the church was non-politics. Local politics overwhelmed villagers. Their major local source of identity, the village, created uncertainty and trepidation in their lives.

The church and its ethereal focus provided a third option between economic improvement and exploitation. But as the ethnic strictures for participating in local development plans were so strong, only one man successfully used church dedication to beg out of some of the more exploitative development schemes. In not participating, though, this man turned his back on his neighbors, potentially generating a major collective action problem, and risked constructing his church as enabling the shirking of responsibilities.

Contrary to the research on the growth of Evangelism in Latin America that stresses its fragmenting results, this case illustrates how Evangelism can be used at the highly localized level to push for structural change. In this chapter, I explore the rise, coming into power, and rule of the Evangelicals in Huaytabamba, concluding with a critical analysis of how this movement engaged with the larger racialized social structure. What enabled the church to revitalize the community, and what resources did it employ to do so? What distinguished the new village incarnation, and how did it safeguard against the exploitation that had undermined local institutions? And, finally, what challenges does it offer to indigenous racialization?

I argue that the church revitalized the community through a "revolutionary culture first" strategy. This created a self-sustaining group within the village ready to seize local opportunities but also capable of weathering challenging times. As in many other cases, Evangelism succeeded in effecting social change through its ability to quickly and cheaply establish a new local culture and its attendant institutions (Chesnut 1997). This was revolutionary in that its ideology, practices, and organization differed dramatically from the mainstream, creating a dedicated group of adherents with a distinct understanding about the way the world worked and how to change it. But distinct from traditional social movements that emphasize the instrumental rationality of participating to accomplish end goals, the church movement provided the additional substantive rationality of participating for the dynamic and exuberant experiences that participation regularly brought.

The village therein contained an autonomous revolutionary group in its midst. And once the exploitative activities of the civic leaders bankrupted the traditional secular worldview, Evangelism acquired the opportunity to remake the community in its own image. Rather than something entirely new, however, Evangelical community revitalization amounted to a reassertion of village *ethnic* identity, particularly the prioritization of horizontal ties of affinity over vertical ties of fealty. The Evangelical leadership used the trust inhering in church relations to reassert the group mutuality long vested in community identity. The emphasis on brotherhood and anti-corruption in the Evangelical subculture, maintained by its revolutionary rupture from the status quo, revitalized these strong latent desires. In this way, the church helped reconstruct local ethnicity back to working for each other's mutual benefit and away from adhering to the plans of the powerful, and improving the village's overall position within the political economy.

The Evangelical movement initially engaged with the racialized social structure in a similar manner that Damian's schemes had: isolation from the urban power center provided the means for this novel ideology to take root. The church eventually existed peacefully within Damian's developmentalist hegemony because it presented neither a threat nor a possibility for exploitation. Developmentalism's precipitous decline provided the opportunity for local Evangelical church-derived governance. And the political and economic wellbeing of villagers improved as a result. Economically, the evangelically derived ethnic governance softened the blow of racialized exploitation: the church provided intermediaries vested in village wellbeing rather than kickbacks, but who still had to provide village participants into the exploitative developmentalist machinery. That is, this new ethnic governance provided a highly conflicted intermediation that attempted to resolve this conflict in favor of the village as much as possible. Politically, though, the new governance created the most meaningful form of participation that the village had ever seen. The challenge beyond this point centered on creatively overcoming institutionalized segregation by making meaningful *external* economic, political, and cultural connections.

EVANGELICAL SOCIAL CHANGE

The rapid, large-scale Evangelical Protestant conversions throughout Latin America inspired scholars into a heated debate between "monolithic portraits" about the nature of this movement (Smilde 2003). Did it amount to widespread egalitarian social change or a revitalization of old forms of domination? Interest in this subject waned, however, as a general consensus emerged that Evangelism's highly decentralized nature largely enabled its rapid spread. This meant that the conversions never cohered into a major society-changing movement, but rather remained highly splintered, with the new religious practices amounting to anything to anyone, depending on their local context and application (Kamsteeg 1998). Herein rides the legacy of the Apostle Paul: "I have become all things to all men, so that I may by all means save some" (1 Corinthians 9:22).

Evangelism's greatest impacts have been highly localized and diverse (Freston 2001). Investigations of this impact confront a laundry list of potential means, outcomes, and limitations to localized change. Researchers must therefore contextualize their findings and implications (Robbins 2004). Outcomes depend on local conditions. And any analysis of larger meanings must control for these conditions. The following section discusses the major impacts of Evangelism in Latin America and their contradictory outcomes in order to contextualize the changes in Huaytabamba.

All sociopolitical change stems in some way from the cultural transformations at the core of Evangelical doctrine and practice. Evangelism emphasizes rupture from the prevailing culture. Its charismatic speaking in tongues rituals, ascetic code, and a dualistic demonizing of the mainstream help it sustain this discontinuity (Robbins 2004, 127). Conversion generates a self-reinforcing community that helps maintain membership and the institution itself (Lim and Putnam 2010). Its emphasis on the laity serving as officers has enabled it to quickly and inexpensively create the institutions through which it operates (Chesnut 1997). Combined, Evangelism has proven a highly transportable culture, dialoguing with rather than superseding local issues. In fact, the Evangelical ability to build institutions, particularly in areas of relative deprivation, greatly enhances its popular appeal. With newly established cultural practices reinforced by strong institutions, Evangelism represents a great potential for further changes.

One of the most dramatic and direct changes, documented in a wide variety of situations, involves a renegotiation of patriarchy. Evangelical strictures—against drinking, adultery, gambling, and fighting—cut men off from traditional areas of status competition that frequently prove abusive to women. Moreover, the new churches have many managerial positions available to women, enabling them to acquire leadership skills and expectations. And Evangelism has reprioritized family life for men. Nevertheless, most teachings emphasize that wives should obey their husbands as the men obey God. And men continue to hold most of the highest positions. Politically, such shifts have enabled broader political participation (Brusco 1993), and have even feminized community political priorities (Burdick 1993).

Looking directly at political change, some researchers find that the origins, structures, practices, and content of the new Protestant churches are inherently and irredeemably authoritarian. Reliance on charismatic leaders and the necessity of church survival all work to reproduce the despotic corporatism that pervades Latin America (Bastian 1993; Chesnut 1997; 2003; Gaskill 1997; d'Epinay 1967; Moreno 1999). Others observe Evangelism's individual and otherworldly focus pushing a withdrawal from politics. And broad surveys find Evangelicals more easily pushed away from politics under difficult circumstances (Smith and Hass 1997; Steigenga and Coleman 1995; Steigenga 2001).

In different cases, Evangelical practices have created new "open spaces" that enrich civil society and foster greater direct participation (Stoll 1990; Hale 1997). Some converts hear the living word of God telling them to act directly and seize vacant properties (Sánchez 2008). In more general terms, researchers have found that internal church practices and beliefs train believers to be active citizens, breaking them from being clientelist subjects, with the universal charismatic experience in which all practitioners speak directly to God enabling practitioners to easily challenge church and other leaders (Burdick 1993; Stoll 1990). Lacking an inherent political agenda, unlike labor movements, the new religion has supported diverse political projects such as raising incomes, creating a peaceful bastion in civil war, helping put down extremist guerillas, demanding resources from the state, overcoming taxing systems, and fighting racism (Annis 1987; Brusco 1993; Burdick 1992, 1996; del Pino 1996; Green 1993; Martin 1990; Muratorio 1982; Stoll 1993).

Research on the economic impact of Evangelism presents a similarly mixed picture. Employers see converts as particularly free from corruption, but also non-prioritizing of earthly labor (Chesnut 1997; Martin 1990; Maxwell 1998). Ascetic practices can help accumulate some limited capital (Maxwell 1998). And the religion can serve as a critique of capitalism and consumerism (Burdick 1993; Meyer 1995, 1999). In contrast, many individuals join because of Evangelism's U.S. origins, hoping to make lucrative social connections (Garrard-Burnett 1993). And some churches teach that the pious will enjoy material prosperity (Coleman 2000; Freston 1995). Overall, Evangelical conversion reliably tightens up household economies by repressing male status expenditures but has no widespread demonstrable elevator for upward mobility.

In sum, Evangelical conversion most generally amounts to a dramatic cultural change and the forging of a new community of practitioners. These changes have variously altered social, political, and economic relations. While some instances have worked towards greater equality, retrenching old forms of domination has also occurred. Looking at individual cases remains one of the best routes for understanding the impact of Evangelism given its splintered nature and engagement with local issues.

Among these many items, the Huaytabamba case engages most directly with the quick, cheap, and rupture-induced creation of a self-sustaining community, and the relation of anti-corruption mandates to fostering more inclusive governance. And Rowan Ireland's (1999) framework provides a guide for analyzing the sociopolitical impact of Huaytabamba conversion. Generalizing across a variety of cases, Ireland argues that the more that spiritualism (1) steers practitioners away from corruption, and (2) into networks confronting the pathologies of poverty, the more the church enriches democratic practices. In the context of Huaytabamba, these variables measure the success of Evangelical governance by evaluating the extent to which it differs from the traditional paternalistic model, including any altered economic standings. Towards this end, I now turn to the origins of Evangelism in the village.

THE EVANGELICAL RISE

Evangelism emerged in Huaytabamba largely because it allowed people to depart from the local Catholic mainstream, particularly the self-destructive elements of heavy drinking, fighting, and domestic abuse. Indeed, violence emerging from Catholic culture has an almost ritualistic aspect to it. Once, I attended a multi-village carnival celebration in the pastures above Huaytabamba. As it got dark and most people began departing, the villagers I had come with insisted on staying. "You should wait here for the fights," they instructed mischievously. Sure enough, as darkness settled different groups of men started yelling at each other. Punching quickly followed. One group successfully surrounded a man, kicked him and beat him on the head with a glass bottle until he lay subdued on the grass, blood coating his face and clothes. My companions just laughed. At the village level, domestic abuse occurred regularly. Don Pedro, later a highly dedicated village pastor, was almost kicked out of the village because his violence became too frequent and too extreme—though he told me he could not remember much of these events.

But the story of the first church begins with illness. One village patriarch, don Alfonso, in desperation turned to some brothers from another village when he could find no other remedy for his colic. Becoming cured, he converted into an ardent believer, undergoing a massive personality transformation through adhering to Evangelical behavioral prescriptions. As the current pastor explained, Alfonso had been notoriously abusive, "had been really wicked, drunk, and crazy; and after conversion he calmed down." During one drunken tirade, he ripped his wife's earlobe from her head. It dangled as a living testament to the violence surrounding particular Catholic-associated practices in Andean life.

In some ways, both Catholicism and Evangelism represented different responses to village impoverishment. Some aspects of the Catholic route, though, clearly exacerbated these conditions by increasing local excess morbidity and mortality. The Evangelical option reacted to these Catholic pathologies. Neither, however, immediately confronted the structural conditions that, in Alfonso's case, prevented real medical treatment from being a viable primary option. Indeed, these conditions made Alfonso desperate enough to experiment with Evangelism. And, some ten years later, Alfonso died a horrible death, screaming throughout the night because he could not get medical treatment for tuberculosis—even though a health post stood less than three kilometers away.

With his initial miracle cure, however, Alfonso became one of the first local converts. He founded the village church and, seen as a living testimony of the truth of the Evangelical worldview, proselytized heavily. His personal turn from self-destructive habits became strong evidence for the efficacy of the radical doctrine that dedication brings salvation—or the more quotidian version of dedication improving the believer's life. This thereby provided Evangelism an inborn reinforcement mechanism: as people adopted the Evangelical culture, they began to lead more healthy lives, inspiring broader dedication to the church. But the interpretation remained in fully Evangelical terms:

> According to the Word which God explains to us, only through faith and believing in God can we become cured and will He cure us from sickness. So we see the brothers that were very sick and that could not get well and with nothing they were cured; with this we believe there exists the power of God.

Believers generalized from their extreme cases[3] of domestic violence and sickness to extend the formula to all other troubles of people's lives, unashamedly exploiting this connection in their attempts to expand the church. Proselytizers maintained that, since Evangelism did not specify any one malady, the formula was universally applicable, whether the problem was a lost cow or cancer. Since these minor successes required a radical universal doctrine, the agents were, in a sense, correct: in order to make the actual changes, in order to make the cultural leap, people had to believe that all changes are possible through the exact same means.

The converts applied their new worldview to everybody's problems, warning that they would get worse, and that the only remedy was Evangelism. They claimed that almost any ailment was fatal, requiring not only the dedication of the sick, but also of the entire family. In one of many instances, a man who had swollen hands from tending cows in high, cold pastures relayed that "don Alfonso said to me 'enter Evangelism because this sickness you have will enter your heart and you can die; but in Evangelism you will be healthy.'" And church authorities preyed on other maladies besides poor health care. One woman explained how the pastor convinced her to become more dedicated to the church. Regarding her poor attendance and participation,

> he told me I would suffer a lot, that something bad was going to happen to me; "it could be the death of your husband or another serious thing." . . . After he told me this, about three days went by and all my animals were stolen.

Because of the pastor's words, the woman easily interpreted her problems as at least partially resulting from her failings as an Evangelical. And, even though I did not necessarily ask for them, well over half of active churchgoers related similar instances about the level of their dedication. Another woman said "we thank God because He gives us what we need; for this I feel what happened to me was a miracle because if I had not remembered God I would not have a cow and I would be wanting to drink milk and eat cheese." Thus, as long as people faced difficult conditions, the church had a vibrant tool for recruiting and retention.

THE EVANGELICAL WORLDVIEW

With the popularity of Evangelism, an apocalyptic worldview pervaded the village. This ideology entailed interrelated ethereal and a mundane perspectives. On the celestial scale, the pre-millenarian grand narrative held that the deteriorating conditions in the world indicated immanent Armageddon, and the signs of the apocalypse were everywhere, one believer explaining:

> Our God Jesus Christ said that for the second coming there will be signals; there will be many wars between nation and nation . . . there will be earthquakes in many places, there will be famines in many places mostly where they do not accept Christ and in these places they will suffer pestilences; and it says as well that in the last days many will grow cold; that is, many believers will chill to the church; and at the moment there are few believers; we analyze and this could be due to the coming of the Lord and for the end of the world.

However, because the signs were literally everywhere, this dynamic could also be applied to everyday life. Any shortcoming was seen in terms of dedication to the church. For example, one woman said

> I am not always happy; rather I am always pensive; I think a lot about the problem that has happened to me with my daughter [she was raped and the Huaytabamba perpetrator refused to take responsibility] and I think this problem is perhaps due to not being at prayers in the temple; and I think that for this maybe I have been castigated for being a single mother, and now that I have my lover (*conviviente*) I am made to suffer.

But people also interpreted almost any gain as a miracle and a reason for further dedication to the church.

Apocalyptism, secular or religious, is generally portrayed as a means to acquire dedicated adherents whose righteousness enables them to persevere against continual setbacks (Roberts 1995). But that the Huaytabamba villagers could immediately apply the material aspect of the doctrine to their everyday lives provided the strongest tool for recruitment and retention. Indeed, because people experienced concrete results, the apocalyptism became more of a liability as the projected end of the world in 2000 never occurred. The key was concrete results. The apocalyptic vision only seemed to provide the main causal relationship for the formula people applied universally to their lives. Apocalyptism did not even seem a major element in the revolutionary rupture, especially in comparison to the rituals, popular empowerment, and other benefits outlined below.

THE EVANGELICAL REVOLUTION

Beyond a universally applicable formula, dedicated adherents, and overcoming Catholic-associated excesses, Evangelism also thrived because it successfully competed with existing *secular* worldviews. Villagers struggled to find good health care, income, and protection against violence in the institutions of the urban-centric world. For example, a woman who had been raped said: "I filed a complaint according to the law believing in the law; but there is not justice." Therefore, Evangelicals could easily interpret sickness, robbery, violence, and economic windfalls in religious rather than secular terms. That is, Evangelism prospered because villagers could not access urban institutions.

As documented elsewhere (cf. Robbins 2004), Evangelism possessed a self-reinforcing appeal by providing a community of like-minded individuals safely enjoying the dynamic practices of their new culture. As found in other places (d'Epinay 1967; Burdick 1993), villagers attended because they enjoyed attending. "I like the singing and the praying," said a typical practitioner. That is, people enjoyed attending services, continually coming because it was substantively rational for them to do so. As the congregation grew, the locale for engaging in wondrous spiritual activities started to became a new focus of village socializing. Perhaps more profoundly, people found that the church gave them new, more fulfilling life priorities: "With Evangelism we are with our families and I am more united with my children and I always think of my family." Further, people looked to the church to solve many of their everyday problems. One woman "prayed to God to get a cow," and thus considered the easy loan from her father-in-law a miracle. That is, seeing posi-

tive "consequences" from their participation, villagers had instrumental-
ly rational reasons for participating.

And one of the most valuable aspects of church life was that it enabled
an escape from the tension and uncertainty of daily life, particularly as
Damian pulled more money out of the village. Damian had tried to head
the Evangelical church just as he tried to control all local institutions.
However, as Damian's younger brother admitted to me, "my brother
wanted to be pastor, but we would not have him." The church proved the
only major institution resilient to Damian's manipulation. As one man
explained it to me, people were elected pastor based almost exclusively
on their dedication to Evangelism. Damian's unparalleled skills, which
had gained him a leadership role throughout the rest of the village, were
rather based in his abilities to engage with the outside world. He did not
wish to meet the onerous time demands of proving church dedication.
The congregation's interests were very insular, focusing almost exclusively on what went on inside the chapel, thereby neutralizing Damian's
appeal.

In sum, with its universally applicable doctrine, successful demonstrations—especially compared to competing worldviews—its dramatic
break from the mainstream culture, heavy persecution, peaceful environment, and active incorporation of all subscribers, Evangelism in Huaytabamba represented a revolutionary change. Rather than incrementally
altering different facets of social life for churchgoers, it transformed all
major aspects of their lives. These changes largely did not challenge villager structural constraints, but simply employed their limited resources
differently.

EVANGELISM TAKES CHANGE

With Damian's sudden departure in 1994 marking the failure of traditional secular institutions, the role of the church began to shift outwards.
In effect, the church began to apply its universal doctrine to the social
institutions of the village rather than restricting it to individual behaviors. This was particularly true once the church stalwarts began filling the
community leadership vacuum, motivated by their Evangelical beliefs to
serve their brothers and sisters. Evangelism bled into the community:
brothers and sisters became fellow community members, not just fellow
believers.

The man the community had earlier wished to exile because of his
abusive drunken behavior, Pedro, stood out among the new leaders. Religion inspired these individuals to take a village leadership position, just
as has occurred throughout Latin America (Garrard-Burnett 1993). "I
want to do something for my brothers and sisters," Pedro explained to
me, so "I have always tried to serve in a [community] office." But the

church also provided a different hierarchy to acquire status and leadership positions. Damian lacked sufficient Evangelical status because he did not prove himself dedicated to the church. In contrast, Pedro and others distinguished themselves through working for the church. "The people admire don Pedro; he is always at services; he always helps; he is a good Christian."

Pedro thus simultaneously held the positions of church pastor and community president from 1998 to 2000. As president and pastor, Pedro revitalized moribund village abilities to engage in community projects. A few people, such as don Alfonso, criticized Pedro for politicizing the pastorship. And several Catholics complained that Evangelical rule undermined the village, some going as far as saying it "brought us disorder even for the dead."

The vast majority, however, regarded Pedro as one of the most effective presidents in village history. With few exceptions, church stalwarts praised him for his political work. And four-fifths (twelve out of fifteen) of the Catholics I spoke with about the issue similarly commended Pedro. As one put it, "in his period [Pedro] achieved many works; he did more works than any recent president; others could not gain the support of the community." These programs included community-wide outhouses, a new school, metal roofing materials for the entire community, a children's food program, and revitalization of the potable water system. In this, Pedro said he would never hate Damian because Damian taught him how to access such resources from urban agencies. Just as under Damian, however, villagers still relied on Pedro as a single intermediary with outsized powers—though he had more pro-village motivations.

Besides religion inspiring Pedro into civic service, he saw civil projects as serving church needs. For instance, he told me that he acquired the outhouses for the village so visiting brothers would have a place to go. For him, there was little dividing the church and the community. And as pastor-president, he blended these institutions even more strongly. Inside the church itself, Pedro "always admonished the congregation [in services] and in this way got the members of the church to rise up and contribute to the community." Pedro used the pulpit to push believers into doing their civic duties and participate in community events and work parties. For him, the village was a family and good Christians must work with and on behalf of their family. And he himself worked hard for the community, soliciting multiple urban institutions for projects.

Pedro's techniques appeared to work. The entire village—now majority Evangelical—once again worked on community projects and in each other's fields. But Pedro not only relied on the perseverance of church subculture and bonds of trust, he exploited it. Pedro fused the church and the village, and employed the recently created church network for tasks formerly under community auspices. In a major instance, Pedro easily convinced both Catholics and Evangelicals alike to knock down the Catholic chapel in order to make room for a new school. Only years later, when a new chapel failed to materialize, did villagers complain about being manipulated. "The Evangelists destroyed our church. . . . Yes, I helped knock it down; but they said a new one would be built and this has not come," one man among many exclaimed. Thus, tying the church and village so closely together successfully overcame historical problems within the community, but ran a serious risk of having narrower religious priorities trump general village needs.

These changes, however, represent more than the revitalization of communal work parties. Such collective labor is a principal component of Andean identity and culture (Allen 1988; Flores Galindo 1988; Gose 1994; Isbell 1978; Mayer 1985). In Huaytabamba, Damian's machinations caused villagers to identify the community with their exploitation and degradation. Now, however, through Pedro fusing the Evangelical subculture to the community, villagers associated community membership with fulfilling the promises of development. In essence, Pedro helped recast the community-based ethnic identity as one of mutuality rather than exploitation. The key to this transformation was the Evangelical church. Specifically, the church provided important *local* measures of success. These were initially just inside the congregation and concerning dedication to the church. However, Pedro's actions expanded these measures to embrace much more of the community. Success became more understood in terms of building the village infrastructure and working with fellow villagers.

EVANGELICAL IMPACT

The success of Evangelically-inspired governing largely depends on its ability to (1) steer practitioners away from corruption and (2) into networks confronting the pathologies of poverty (Ireland 1999). Regarding the former, Pedro's regime still engaged with the highly corrupt paternalist agencies responsible for rural resource distribution, but largely prevented them from cycling into a means of wealth extraction as occurred under Damian.

The case of constructing the school illustrates the characteristics and limits of these anti-corruption activities. Fujimori's patronage machine, the Ministry of the Presidency, made the funds for the school available (Gonzales de Olarte 1998). Similarly, the district mayor awarded the school as a quid-pro-quo for villager votes. The edifice, however, promised no educational improvements, simply replacing the old adobe school with one made of the "noble materials" of cement and brick. Further, as one aid worker put it, "the mayor got them all to vote for him and now this school is flooded [with water]." The benefaction proved useless as ten inches of stagnant water covered its floors.

This project was tied directly to the patronage mechanisms of the state. And the Evangelical character of local government influenced the decision to knock down the Catholic chapel and use the civic institutions to advance a religious agenda. Nevertheless, the project was positive in that it gained resources for the village and helped people work together again. The other projects, such as road building and new metal roofing, were not so fatally flawed. The orange outhouses and the orange bowls of the children's meal program, however, matched the color of Fujimori's party, the projects advertising his generosity. Like the school, these Huaytabamba public works came directly from the presidential patronage machine.

Economically, the Evangelical government undid the worst facets of developmentalist exploitation. Indeed, the Evangelical church enabled Pedro to navigate the structural tensions between development and exploitation in a new way. The anti-corruption stance stopped leaders from using projects to acquire personal wealth. Combined with the individualized character of village power, this translated into preventing the overtly exploitative aspects of development from entering the village. In so doing, this new form of leadership considerably improved the village's position within the exploitative political economy. These successes played on the contradiction between Fujimori's cheap vote-getting machine and more regional forces interested in leveraging these funds into fortifying their extractive clientelist networks. Pedro was able to achieve a net gain from urban resources—in contrast to the precipitous losses under Damian—though at the cost of fairly ubiquitous Fujimori propaganda and popularity.

Regarding Ireland's (1999) second issue of positive networking, the civil war had seriously stifled social movements, including those of an indigenous character, leaving little opportunity for networking (Garcia and Lucero 2004; Yashar 2005). Under Pedro's regime, however, the village did successfully confront a growing right wing movement. Part of Fujimori's neoliberal reforms included the 1995 Land Law advocating the privatization of village land tenure systems and creating land markets in the name of efficiency (Ministerio de Agricultura 2004). Such a change, as has occurred in other areas and earlier in Peru's history, would mean— and even advocates—a regressive redistribution of land and power (Spalding 1975; Ministerio de Agricultura 2004). This would increase the resources available for extraction by local paternalist networks. Instead of Huaytabamba villagers entrusting the moneys from selling their animals as occurred in the 1980s, villagers could be forced to take out loans or even sell their lands, therein losing the primary basis of their reproduction and making them more dependent upon the locally powerful.

The four most powerful families, considered the founders of the village, pushed the privatization effort. Three of the four patriarchs were Evangelical, including don Alfonso. The remaining thirty-six families desired to preserve the *comunidad campesina* system that protected lands from taxation and expropriation, and helped villagers access labor and external resources. While the patriarchs presented privatization as a means to make lands more valuable and secure, all the others viewed it as threatening their livelihoods.

Under Pedro, the village dispatched this threat in a straightforward and formal way, demonstrating the kind of new governance brought through Evangelical revitalization. Previously, Damian's schemes mainly fleeced villagers through relying on the various informal, clientelistic networks that can rule over the countryside with little *de jure* authority—including Damian himself who frequently acted on behalf of the village without holding any official capacity. Pedro's regime, in contrast, insisted that the privatization decision must occur through the formal governing mechanisms of the village. As the patriarchs visited individuals in their homes and tried to convince villagers of the value of privatizing, Pedro called the matter up for vote at a general comunidad meeting in 1998. Villagers rejected the motion en masse and the issue faded from people's concerns.

That is, through bolstering the major comunidad institutions, Evangelical revitalization prevented the locally dominant from using their high status, resources, and powerful external allies to intimidate or otherwise persuade reluctant villagers. By placing the matter in the official arena for debate and decision-making—the general assembly—Pedro's regime further strengthened village institutions through staving off a direct threat to them. This method did not stifle dialogue, but rather enabled the kind of egalitarian discourse that research on participatory governance says is essential for empowered citizenship (Baiocchi 2001; Nylen 2003; Evans 2004; Wampler 2004, 2007; Dijkstra 2005; Morrison and Singer 2007).

In contrast to the highly individualized intermediation of development projects, the privatization struggle demonstrated a diffuse and democratic power. The fellowship and anti-corruption strictures translated into participatory governance. Rather than breaching the rural-urban divide, this democracy relied on staying within the confines of the segregated community. Staving off village exploitation entailed keeping issues under the auspices of robust village institutions and preventing the powerful from leveraging their external connections to supersede local decision-making processes. The church thus helped provide an empowered alternative to the normal despotic form of rural authority, and as such fended off regressive structural adjustments.

CREATIVE RESISTANCE

Mass Evangelical conversions can have dramatic political consequences. But these impacts have been disparate and localized, not enabling broad social movements or easy academic generalizations. In Huaytabamba, church participation meant many things to many people. The most far-reaching political impact, though, entailed a renegotiation of ethnicity. This in turn revitalized the collective decision-making infrastructure of the village, resulting in enhancing the overall position of the village within the political economy.

The church created a vibrant, self-sustaining, and revolutionary local subculture ready to seize local opportunities to assert long-standing popular priorities around group mutuality. In the church, all interested people could participate fully; and the vibrant rituals' unpredictable events enticed people to come. With the new institution thus quickly established and cheaply sustained, it became a safe venue for otherwise stymied forms of camaraderie, and a new center for village social life.

In the village, the strong discourse of local ethnic mutuality remained latent, even after it had been terribly exploited. People believed in it and wanted it to happen. But their recent experiences made them not understand how it could. The church's fraternal ideology kept the spark of ethnic affinity alive, and spread it once Evangelical forces took civil power. The church provided new community leadership unwilling to benefit from and thereby perpetuate the corruption through which Damian had previously extracted windfall resources.

More profoundly, these leaders provided a novel means to employ the village's limited resources and differently navigate local structural constraints. Following the anti-corruption, fraternal Evangelical ideology helped reinvigorate the principal means of democratic participation and accountability. By so valuing village-level organizations, the church challenged the individual exercise of power pushed by the shape of governing institutions. Accountability remained non-institutionalized: a single villager still served as representative to the urban core, accountable only to the village institutions because of his Evangelical beliefs. But this enabled the village to fend off the extractive impulses of the development industry and the regressive privatization movement, resulting in an improved overall position for the village within the political economy. As I will show in the next chapter, this new governance provided the best resource for asserting villagers' will in the face of a regenerated and highly coercive privatization movement. Its failures to make meaningful external connections across the village's situation of institutionalized segregation, however, resulted in its eventual demise.

NOTES

1. This chapter is a revised version of Scarritt (2013).
2. While Pentecostal would be the most correct social scientific categorization of these sects, believers and critics alike regularly employ the term Evangelical. As with major journals focused on Latin America, I follow this vernacular usage.
3. The successes were extreme in the fact that they were akin to "curable illnesses," untreated due to the pathologies of the prevailing system, particularly the hard living brought through the self-destructive behaviors encouraged by that system.

Looking over Huaytabamba village square down toward Ayacucho.

The surprising and nefarious tractor and the hills behind the village.

Children greeting us on our arrival in front of the Casa Comunal.

An arduous *ayni* of turning over the earth by hand in coordinated groups.

Damian dominating a meeting and insisting on the sanctity of paperwork.

Converting to Evangelism at the creek on the edge of Huaytabamba during a two-day festival.

A town of two presidents: comunidad president (foreground) arguing with the private president.

Small and deteriorating irrigation infrastructure in a picturesque location.

The Mothers' Club sponsored cleaning of the village square with the defunct school in the background.

The author in the field. Photograph courtesy of Jill Lawley.

FIVE

Racially Reinventing Privatization

On a brisk sunny day in 2003, I visited Damian at his house in Huayta-bamba. Damian had mysteriously returned to the village in 2000. He had walked down from the highway pass above the village where the Lima bus had dropped him off. He lacked money, personal belongings, and even his national identity card. The common story ran that he had been with another woman and:

> This woman searched through his bag, saw his documents and his money and kicked him out. . . . She took everything. In Huamanga [Ayacucho city] he borrowed money and his jacket from his grand-father, and with this he came. . . . With one outfit no more he came; his wife sold a bull and with this bought him his clothes.

Not surprisingly, nobody was happy to see him. "We are Evangelicals and have learned to overcome; if we were Catholics we would garrote him," commented one man. Another said, seeing that his earlier disap-pearance did not mark his death, "the devil is going to take him and burn him. . . . There he will pay for all his sins and when he burns he will stay as ashes and coal."

Despite his diminished standing and poor reception, Damian soon began spearheading a new privatization movement. As noted in the last chapter, the villagers had soundly rejected privatization when it was pro-posed at a regular community meeting, with only four of thirty-six fami-lies desiring it. Damian had decided not to settle for the popular will and began reviving the privatization issue.

My visit to Damian's house occurred in the midst of his privatization campaign. He sat me outside on a rock covered by a sheep's hide in his small muddy yard, surrounded by short raw adobe buildings and a list-ing stockade. I drank heavily sweetened herbal tea from a battered blue enamel cup while Damian rummaged inside his darkened house. Finally joining me in the cool mountain sunshine, Damian flourished a stunted pencil and wrote out twin lists of names on small scraps of paper. I knew and regularly engaged with everyone on the first list because they lived in the village. I did not know most of the people on the second list, though, because they were rarely if ever in Huaytabamba.

Much to my astonishment, Damian explained to me that all of the villagers I knew actually had no legitimate say in community government, including the current officeholders themselves. They were non-qualified (*no calificado*) individuals, people supposedly forbidden from village political participation. The other list recorded the names of the people he believed were qualified (*calificado*) community members, people who had legitimately fulfilled the requirements to participate. He claimed that only these people could make the rules governing the village.

This was an astoundingly ridiculous claim. It flew directly against the laws and practices governing comunidades. These explicitly state, for instance, that qualification requires primary residence in the village.[1] More practically, those on Damian's qualified list could not fulfill the core comunidad requirements of (1) providing labor for all faenas and other village projects, and (2) attending the comunidad meetings, the very entity that Damian claimed they commanded. In fact, these same individuals endlessly complained that the requirements made comunidad membership far too onerous for them. Thus, while Damian clothed his claim in legalese, the flesh of the matter stood naked. All the urban-dwelling people on the qualified list wanted to privatize the land. Anti-privatization village residents, in contrast, made up the non-qualified list. If Damian could somehow make his absurd assertion stick, privatization would become reality.

These lists and their ridiculousness show the nature of Damian's privatization campaign. Rather than seeking a positive popular vote by convincing people based on the merits of privatization itself, Damian employed thinly veiled fraud and intimidation in an attempt to impose privatization against villagers' wills. Privatization no longer centered on people's choice. Instead it became a hostile struggle in which the few pitted their superior resources against the desires of the many. And Huaytabamba therein launched itself into the newest incarnation of the dilemma that has kept the indigenous subordinated for so long: the Neoliberal Indian Question.

THE NEOLIBERAL INDIAN QUESTION

Starting in the early 1990s, Peru implemented some of the fastest and farthest reaching neoliberal reforms. Enhanced global market integration and the slashing of social spending, combined with increased access to local lands, generated a boom in extractive resources like gold and natural gas. Not surprisingly, only a small group partook of the windfalls, with less than five percent of the population enjoying any rise in income. And wealth became much more concentrated.

Feeding the opportunities provided by these speculative booms exacerbated the national elite's traditional dilemma of having to incorporate ever greater territory into extraction in order to maintain economic dominance and social control. The greatest conflicts of this era surrounded providing multinational corporations with territories already claimed and used for non-extractive activities like farming and living. Famously, the President of the Republic, Alan García, penned an editorial deriding smaller landholders as the fabled dog in the manger: the cur spitefully preventing others from having resources he cannot himself use. García harkens back to the old cultural exchange racial trope of Juan de Matienzo (see chapter 2) that bringing civilization justifies the pillage of conquest, or its more recent developmentalist incarnation claiming Europeans use resources better than Indians.[2]

Neoliberalism also presents a new cultural dilemma. Moving away from developmentalism based on a single, mestizo, national identity, neoliberalism's embrace of the global market is inherently multicultural, equating distinctions more with positive market differentiation than negative impediments to growth (Hale 2002). As the global market creates new opportunities for elite windfalls, it simultaneously undermines the traditional exclusionary practices based on cultural assimilation.

Considered together, these twin dilemmas present a new version of the Indian Question: how can elites leverage racial difference in order to prime national territory for potential rendering to multinational corporations? The answer is mestizo multiculturalism, a strain in which the diversity inherent in mestizaje is made to meet the needs of both national political pressures and those of global integration. As Drinot (2011, 187) shows at the national level, this is a violent and much more overtly racist retrofitting of the state mestizaje project, demonizing the indigenous in order to tap "into an essential or primitive fear in Peru." The internal stresses of mestizaje are exacerbated rather than resolved.

In particular, as dispossession-driven growth makes more people superfluous to the global economy, neoliberalism must be harnessed to control the excluded. Rather than diffusing tension through new forms of token inclusiveness as has occurred in other countries, mestizo multiculturalism retrenches racism, reconstructing social institutions to more directly serve mestizo interests at the expense of the Indian.

This is more than the scapegoat role natives played in explaining the failure of national development. In this model, they have no place in the nation, neither ideologically nor in providing a source for low wage labor. Neoliberalism finally presents an answer to the vexing question that has plagued coloniality throughout its five hundred year history: how to gain windfall profits without the bitter dependency on indigenous labor? As chapter 2 showed, colonials regularly undermined their own wellbeing by eroding the native labor pools upon which they depended—generally through genocidal means. Neoliberalism promises to free them of this constraint.

As Saskia Sassen points out, this is a logic of expulsion that undergirds our system of advanced financial capitalism. Neoliberalism concentrates wealth under conditions of weak growth through accumulation by dispossession—through taking things rather than making things (Harvey 2005). This creates the problem (among many others) of needing ever more expansive (rather than intensive) forms of growth, the appropriation of more and diverse things into capitalist circuits: "finance needs to invade—that is, securitize—nonfinancial sectors to get the grist for its mill" (Sassen 2014, 9). Beyond simple privatization, financial logic seeks to create markets and commodities where none existed before, such as in education and health care, attempting to render everything down to the universally fungible concept of debt.

And, "at the center of this logic," Sassen (2012, 75) explains,

> is not the "valuing" of people as workers and consumers, but the expulsion of people and the destruction of traditional capitalisms to feed the needs of the new capitalism, one dominated by the interests of high finance and the needs for natural resources.

Rather than needing to exploit people to increase productivity, financial logic expels people who are now simply in the way of incorporating ever more resources into financial circuits. Advanced financial capitalism thus depends on "a savage sorting of winners and losers" whereby great windfalls accrue to the few while rendering the majority superfluous to capitalism, and marked for expulsion or worse (Sassen 2010). Moreover, this breaks in heavily racialized ways, the winners mostly white and the losers mostly darkly complected (Robinson 2013). But before this can happen, the valence of these things must be changed so that they can be rendered appropriable by capital. This is a messy and conflict riven process.

Important questions in these transformations still need significant addressing, especially as applies to the Huaytabamba case. In particular: how does expulsion occur? More precisely, how do resources become transformed for potential appropriation by financial capital? Note that this is a question of *potential* rather than actual appropriation. The distinction is important because it amounts to bearing the costs of holding a resource until financial capital can engineer a value for it. So this is a double issue: (1) the valence of the resource needs to be altered so as to become immediately appropriable by capital once capital finds a value for it, but (2) capital needs to externalize the cost of maintaining the resource in that condition until it has a value. This is the logic of the casino economy: resources need to be converted into financial poker chips and held as such until the very rare moment that financial capital creates the right high-stakes game through which it can gain outsized returns — arbitrage.

Beyond the conquistadors' gold lust, strange windfalls from global markets have actually, if rarely, occurred in the Andes. Booms in such things as cochineal, quinoa, wool, and lithium feed dreams and the market development of a huge range of mostly frustrated products. In all of these, and even more localized variations such as spikes in prices of Andean squashes due to coca booms, capricious external demand drives the price fluctuations. Other more fully non-local dynamics have created similar opportunities for the third world, such as speculative food markets inspiring corporations and foreign countries to try and capture large tracts of lands for food or other commodity production. Or the new liquidity can be poured into even greater pyramid schemes than those under developmentalism (Stoll 2013). So playing the global market lottery means being primed for the unexpected: render yourself immediately available for any peculiar demand. The global market can provide fantastic if rare windfalls, with the local needing to condition itself for financial capital as a necessary but far from sufficient condition for realizing this capricious largess.

Clearly there are many different processes that can work towards this same end of financial deepening, moderated by local conditions. Sassen (2010) refers to these as "systemic equivalents." Yet there may be more equivalence in these than different local evocations of financial logic, or at least some underexplored avenues to better hone in on the subterranean dynamics driving these remarkably similar, widespread, and relatively rapid transformations. While not seeking a definitive or all encompassing process, this chapter argues for the centrality of race in enabling neoliberal transformations. In general, the *racial* dynamics of coloniality enable the success of the neoliberal *class* project. Stewart Hall's (1980, 394) famous words acquire a new potency: "Race is the modality in which class is lived."

More specifically, the extremity of neoliberal policies strains the extant racialized social hierarchy. While bottom-rung groups face shocking deprivations in our planet of slums, middle stratum positions confront an unprecedented downward mobility. With its stark choice between fantastic windfalls or terrifying loss, the neoliberal casino economy recruits these middle groups to do its bidding lest they become victims themselves. This process occurs through forging a much more overt racism, both in terms of ideologically constructing othered groups' interests as irrational, and institutionalizing social relations that render such groups disposable. By concentrating power, this new racism enables the imposition of financial logics: the altering of resource valences to make them appropriable to and held in reserve for incorporation into financial circuits. In Peru, the unbridled racism of President García, openly equating Indians with spiteful dogs because they did not want to concede their resources to international oil interests, speaks to the logics driving the project.

PRIVATIZATION'S STRATEGIC LIE

To address the challenges and possibilities presented by neoliberalism at the village level, Damian eventually settled on a new strategy for his land privatization movement. The campaign abandoned the idea of convincing villagers of the virtue of privatization based on the logic provided by the World Bank or the neoliberal institutions implementing the policies locally. Instead, the privatizers began to try and totally invert villagers' understanding of the legislation. Specifically, the privatizers began insisting that staying with the comunidad actually meant land loss while inscribing into privatization would bring land security.

The privatizers maintained that, through their work with urban organizations, they found out that privatization was going to happen regardless of villager actions. They spelled out privatization as an inexorable technocratic unfolding of urban-based policy. They said that the national government had passed the law. And now the new agencies worked to implement it throughout the countryside. Privatization, they said, was inevitable, and villagers could do nothing to stop it. This new strategy, then, moved from trying to convince villagers of the merit of privatization and therefore vote in its favor, to simply dismissing village self-determination as irrelevant. Villages and their governance had no roles to play.

One of the major consequences of this inevitable privatization, the privatizers stressed, was that villagers trying to stay with the comunidad faced imminent land loss. The explanation for the inevitability of privatization was complex and convoluted. It had to do with a combination of lacking the right kind of paperwork, the process through which villagers initially obtained their lands in the 1960s, and the wording of the new land policies. This meant that the village did not have a true claim on the protections offered by the comunidad system. Additionally, all land transfers made under comunidad auspices were void. Therefore, the original land purchasers—including the deceased, close family members, and people long moved to other locales—were the actual owners of the land. They could, and most likely would, return to claim their property.

The solution to this technical problem, said the privatizers, was not one of political decision-making. Instead, they had to confront it in kind, manipulating the paperwork before the urban agencies started their process. Without properly conditioning the land documentation in the village, the technocratic land market-creating procedure would not count villager lands as their own. Thus, to preserve their lands, villagers would first have to enlist in privatization. Then they would have to work with the privatizers to manufacture a paper trail that showed the current landholders as legitimately possessing the lands through transfers from the original buyers. So the issue for the privatizers became convincing villagers to inscribe.

But the privatizers also sometimes put this in highly personal terms as an outright threat. As Damian's father explained to me: "they do not have papers for their fields so we are going to take their fields." And they regularly went around to people's houses and told them this. The privatizers pushed the impersonal inevitability of privatization and also the personal menace of it. As they claimed they worked to expedite the privatization process, they presented themselves as the agents of expropriation—but also salvation. "For those who do not enroll, they will lose their lands," they explained.

This interpretation was patently false. The personnel at the PETT (the Special Land Titling Project of the Ministry of Agriculture) office responsible for privatization scoffed at it. To the contrary, they intimately knew of the endemic lack of land titles in the sierra. They rather saw their job as formalizing the informal: providing clear titles to the people who actually possessed the lands. They would never impose titles against village practices nor provide titles to non-existent people. The personnel at the public registry similarly denounced this idea as ludicrous, pointing out that dead people could not own lands.

None of the villagers believed it either—at least initially. Yet this interpretation provided the means to eventually have privatization imposed upon the village. This raises important questions: Why lie about privatization? If they had to lie about it, why push privatization so hard? Why this particular lie? And the big question: How did such a poor falsehood successfully leverage privatization?

WHY LIE?

"This model of smallholders without technology is a vicious circle of extreme poverty. We must encourage medium-sized property, the middle class of farmers who know how to obtain resources, seek out markets and create formal jobs."
—President Alan García, 2007

The privatizers needed to lie because the villagers saw privatization as a thorough undermining of the comunidad upon which they depended for their way of life, particularly their access to land that they saw as the core of their reproductive strategies. Born out of the Agrarian Reform, the comunidad system provided villagers access to lands based on participating in village governance and not violating the rules that prevented land re-concentration. Members had to live in the village, not own land elsewhere, serve in offices and committees, provide work when demanded, and attend monthly and extraordinary meetings. Without budgeted external moneys, comunidades had to administer their own infrastructure using villager labor and funds, and donations from urban organizations. Families also coordinated mutual labor exchanges informally through the comunidad. While granted official sanction by the Ministry of Agriculture, the internally elected and unpaid president oversaw external fund acquisition, coordinating faenas, land conflicts, and land transfers. Regularly monthly meetings of the entire village population made governing decisions.

In Huaytabamba meetings, everyone greeted each other vociferously as they trickled in, showing particular deference to the oldest men. They trotted out a rickety wooden table from the school and sometimes some chairs for the president while everyone else sat on the hard-packed ground against the buildings lining the small village square. Men dominated discussions with women once totally forbidden from participating, though sometimes the women would coordinate their voices as a chorus for important issues. Once the meeting ended, everyone who attended signed their names and national identity numbers in the comunidad minutes, with the illiterate stamping their thumb print. While mostly mundane, heated discussions frequently arose about how best to spend scarce comunidad resources, with the president the easy target of discontent.

As the villagers feared, the World Bank and the Ministry of Agriculture, like President García above, openly targeted the comunidad as the paragon of inefficiency and stressed land concentration as the remedy. They advocated for privatization and its increased access to credit precisely because they accelerated land re-concentration. Any such neoliberal argument about a radical redistribution of lands terrified villagers. Ninety percent of households expressed dread of a "return to private property like the hacendados," that "we will all be working just to pay the property tax," or otherwise be squeezed off the lands. Additionally, as one man explained, people feared that under the privatization regime collective work parties of faena and ayni would diminish and eventually disappear. Others said, "if we enter private property . . . we will lose external aid." And many urban authorities concurred. The district mayor, for example, believed that the push to privatize "has to be due to the interests of just a few landholders" because

> If Huaytabamba is going to be a private property and have their individual titles, for this they are going to pay taxes [*tributar*] and they will no longer be assisted by this law of not paying as a Peasant Community; they lose this right.

An agent at the Ministry of Agriculture echoed this, saying the Ministry would no longer oversee private villages so they would lose eligibility for its programs. Thus, the privatizers had to lie about the nature of privatization because everyone else agreed with the villagers that privatization meant the end of comunidad and secure access to land.

MUSTERING THE URBANITES

Given the need to lie, why the big push for privatization? There were many reasons to privatize. The privatizers openly stated that the new land tenure system would *hacer valer*—give value—to the lands. With the restrictions imposed by the comunidad system, the privatizers believed their lands were undervalued. More immediately, they felt they could not adequately leverage their landholdings for loans and other resources. The unfurling of yet another land tenure system on top of the existing ones also potentially further destabilized a rickety system. Only 17 percent of landholders in the entire country have clear title, while well over 90 percent of highland smallholders have no title at all. In Huaytabamba, nobody had clear title to all of their lands, and most had no clear title to any of their plots. The privatizers were thus motivated by the idea of using privatization to acquire clear titles to all village lands. Most villagers rather viewed clear title as an impossible dream.

But this does not explain the privatizers' tenacity, their willingness to use all of their resources to gain privatization at any cost. Rather, the newly empowered city-dwelling and mestizo assimilating made up the force behind the revitalized privatization movement. Privatization uniquely served their interests and promised a massive reorganization of rural spaces to operate according to their economic rationalities. Damian mustered this group as his secret weapon in the privatization struggle.

This was a diverse group of people differently connected to the village. And it was even more so as the violence of the 1980s inspired massive urban immigration, especially among young men, doubling the size of the city of Ayacucho in ten years. Even though institutionalized segregation characterizes highland Peru, people regularly move around. Urban residency, however, does not translate into mestizo access. Access requires cultural capital. Migration is thus highly risky and can only occur through family support. Even simple moves are expensive. The twelve kilometer bus ride to Ayacucho costs villagers ten percent of their daily wage, *each way*. Total relocation, especially to the much more expensive city, entails a major commitment relying on all possible income sources. As with other parts of the world, such migration makes up part of a diversified family income strategy, each potentially subsidizing the other and spreading out risk. For instance, the Aguja family gave one son money to seek work building the natural gas pipeline passing through the Department of Ayacucho on its way from the jungle, over the Andes, and to the coast. While these jobs pay twice the minimum wage, they actually created continual household conflict as many people had claims on parts of the seven dollars a day salary.

Once in the city, village status heavily influences urban success, generally exacerbating rather than overcoming rural differentiation (MacIsaac and Patrinos 1995). Marisol de la Cadena (2000, 182) polarizes these categories between Indigenous Mestizos who succeed by leveraging their rural-urban connections, and denigrated "Urban Indians [who] are unsuccessful immigrants from the countryside." Most eke out a living in the city, variously supplemented by their rural connections. For instance, Damian's brother Antonio, much more comfortable speaking Quechua than Spanish and lacking Damian's relatively privileged background, had worked in many different locales. For his most lucrative job, he had harvested guano on the coast, receiving the relatively high wage of seven dollars for every eighty kilo bag harvested, of which he could do several a day. But he resented that ninety percent of the income from his labor went to others. He had actually used a lot of these wages to expand his landholdings in Huaytabamba, keeping himself closely tied to the village. When he lived in Ayacucho he mostly scrambled for minimum wage manual labor such as loading trucks or construction. Sometimes he speculated on cattle at the market, looking for undervalued animals and buying and selling them at the market on the same day. He lived with his grandfather in a small house along with his wife and five children.

While Antonio generally lived day to day, others had more stable incomes. Some worked in retail sales. Others worked in textiles. There was actually a high demand for maids in Ayacucho and Lima where several of the younger women worked. None of these were particularly lucrative. Most instead fed into larger family strategies that encompassed village agricultural production and farther flung migration such as to the jungle in the dry season or to large cities.

Living in the city, these individuals had been on the periphery of village life—with the exceptions of the ones who played brokerage roles. Most came for part of a day to work their fields at harvest or other important times, while staying away from the village for most of the year. Some only came for brief social visits every year or two, the warmth of their receptions marking their long absences. But they all violated village norms, such as faena and meeting participation. As a result, they had little say in village governance and lived under the potential though never realized threat of having their lands confiscated and redistributed.

For them, Peru's highly polarized economic boom made urban life more precarious. With extractive resource windfalls largely privatized amongst the top one percent, the remainder faced markets saturated with imported goods, slashed social spending, deteriorating infrastructure, and poor job prospects. Even within the booming sectors, foreigners dominated the few white-collar jobs while the manual labor supply outstripped demand and wages remained low.

Their diversified urban-based reproductive strategies became strained. People had to squeeze all of their resources. Under these conditions access to land became more important. And onerous obligations from comunidad regulations became costlier. Luckily, neoliberalism offered an out through the privatization of lands and the dismantling of the comunidad system. Further, with the government and international organizations targeting the comunidad, it proved one of the most accessible routes for easing economic stresses. And, with peculiar booms sporadically erupting in the Andes, it held the potential to provide windfalls.

These individuals had a host of long-standing complaints about comunidad governance. They felt particularly put upon by community meeting and labor obligations. They even put this in terms of fairness, that these burdens fell harder upon them because living in the city made obligations so much costlier to fulfill. They had to pay for the journey to the village. They had to incur greater costs in maintaining themselves in the village, as residents had many more resources at their fingertips since they lived there. Food, tools, labor, pack animals, even knowledge were all easier for villagers to come by. In this, city dwellers complained that the village asked too much: too many meetings and too many faenas. The comunidad had too much say—regulation—over the aspects through which they worked their fields. Access to irrigation, for instance, required participating in canal maintenance that was much easier for villagers with much lower opportunity costs. But also access to labor and the general knowledge of when that labor needed expending was costly to come by, if, for example, they wanted to pay someone to fulfill their obligations for them. Prior to the privatization struggle, they used these issues as rationalizations for not fulfilling comunidad obligations. But as privatization became more of a possibility, these complaints became the guidelines for altering the village.

In Damian's reconceptualization of the village, these individuals moved to playing central roles in village decision-making, and as such sought to have the village more directly serve their urban needs. And the lists that Damian drew up in my opening vignette demonstrated how this process invigorated indirect rule: the new mestizo enfranchisement comes directly through the disenfranchisement of indigenous-associated villagers from even the most trivial aspects of their daily lives.

Thus the Land Law, as the most poignant aspect of neoliberalism for villages, extends well beyond issues of private titles. Rather, it amounts to a racial remaking of rural reality that aligns with the logics of financial capital. Racially, this was a polarized debate about the ethnic valence of the lands. Villagers faced the stark choice between the mutually exclusive options of fields operating to undergird (1) a rural, indigenous-associated reproductive strategy involving access to land partially predicated upon fulfilling certain village-level obligations, or (2) an urban, mestizo-based strategy of independent landholders paying monetized taxes to guarantee private property rights. The latter not only meant the dissolution of the comunidad and the various resources it provided, but also portended a spiral towards landlessness and a feudal-like dependence for actual village residents who did not sufficiently integrate into the urban economy and culture. In other words, the privatization struggle was a struggle to de-Indianize the land, the resource most strongly associated with indigeneity, a struggle for land mestizaje.

Privatization not only heralded a major increase in power for mestizos, it was more specifically a shift from a production-based form of organization to one enabling a whole host of rent-seeking activities, a localized rendering of the accumulation by dispossession that characterizes neoliberalism. While some observers may not find this overly surprising, this case demonstrates the racial nature of the struggle. Freeing the land from comunidad restraints and tying them to urban reproductive strategies meant that exercising these rent-seeking activities became the purview of the culturally assimilated, the mestizos. And, true to the cumulative and circular causality typical of most race relations, the new categories of rentier and renter promised to polarize racial distinctions even more, between the entrepreneurial mestizo and the dependent Indian, making race ever more important.

Finally, this racial remaking of rural spaces aligned with the interests and needs of the larger neoliberal project, in particular rendering village resources much more comprehensible to financial capital and the possibility of gaining windfall profits. Concentrated political control over lands meant quick transferability. Freeing land control from productivity created owners prioritizing monetized profitability, meaning they became highly predisposed to taking offers they deemed profitable. Sharper racial distinctions—alongside the geographic separation to the city of the key village decision-makers—freed landowners of even the most paternalistic feeling of social responsibility, enabling the triumph of let die discourses necessary for dispossession and displacement. Thus, if some spin in the casino economy made financial capital covet these lands, such interests would find them readily and cheaply available. A lowball bid by financial interests would seem a massive windfall in the Andean context.

Damian soon began calling village meetings of this private group, with some participants coming to the village for the first time in years. The comunidad side denounced this new group as lacking any authority. But the comunidad side still tried to work with the private side, saying that a divided village could not work. These regular meetings centered mostly on attending the chores of what they regarded as the privatization process. But they served most directly as a major means of intimidation. Whatever they were doing, they were strategizing with powerful people and this made villagers worried—and justifiably so.

LAND LAW PROMOTED COERCION

The urban constituency urged privatization and the neoliberal logic required a lie. But why did the privatizers settle on the lie that the community meant land loss and privatization land security? Much of this had to do with the way that the new Land Law legislation was actually implemented. As I explain in more detail elsewhere (Scarritt 2010), the enactment as it deviated from the letter of the law shows that, regardless of intention, the PETT provided privatization-minded elites with the means and incentive to racially coerce villagers to privatize.

Most glaringly, the law provided rights for villagers in overtly indigenous ways, supposedly out of respect of traditions going back to "ancient times." Implementation of the law, however, failed to provide a means to exercise these rights, therein embracing the tradition of relegating Indians to right-less subjects rather than citizens, as has occurred for centuries. Instead, the PETT exclusively served privatization interests. In other words, given the polarizing nature of the legislation, the implementation pitted brokers' interests directly against the villagers they were supposedly representing. In this, the privatizers had to find a way to provide the PETT with what it would regard as a legitimate appeal to privatize and be able act on it. And they had to do so within the confines of what the legislation allowed.

To begin at the end, Damian's rather simplistic solution of enrolling in privatization actually comes directly from the PETT. The PETT said it would enter any village that chose to privatize. Once invited to a village, the Ministry planned to bring aerial photographs and provide titles according to (1) who the villagers said owned the lands and (2) any extant land titles. Thus, if the privatizers could present the PETT with documentation showing popular support for privatizing, the PETT would initiate the titling process. In a failed early scheme, Damian circulated a petition in which he seemingly relented on a small local issue. But he removed the last page holding the signatures and attached it to a different document asking the Ministry of Agriculture to privatize local plots, thereby demonstrating a supposed majority in favor of a private land tenure system.

The challenge to providing such documentation, however, centered on getting villagers to accept it so that the PETT could come to the village and demarcate holdings. The PETT refused to engage with local conflicts and would simply demarcate any such fields as contested and therefore without title. Thus, to privatize, elites had to represent the lands as conflict free, including free of acrimony about privatization itself. Damian's falsified petition failed to meet these criteria because villagers readily denounced it.

Luckily for the privatizers, however, the PETT provided them with tremendous leeway. The law specified that communities had to freely choose to privatize through a two-thirds majority. Yet the PETT provided no means, infrastructure, resources, or authority through which villages should make this decision. This stands in marked contrast to the regularization of national elections that strove for transparency through concrete processes monitored nationally and internationally, specifically to prevent the powerful from manipulating the results to serve their interests. Instead, the PETT defaulted to expecting villages to sort out these issues by themselves in whatever way they saw fit. To the extent that the Land Law's two-thirds clause insinuates a free and fair process, the Ministry expected the village to provide the democratic content. In other words, the PETT invited manipulation.

An assumption of mutually aligned village interests and lack of differentiation paralleled this democratic presumption. Without any transparent regulatory mechanism, the PETT assumed that powerful local interests differentially integrated into the larger society did not exist to a sufficient extent to dominate or completely subvert the local decision-making process and use it to enhance their power. Or if they did, the Ministry provided no means to stop it. The Ministry therein defaulted to conferring impunity to local elites in terms of both methods and timeline. The new legislation granted them carte blanche to pursue their interests according to their lights, and for as long as it took them.

Further, the form of law implementation heavily conditioned this process to be coercive, making these elites fully responsible for locally manufacturing the conditions that would enable privatization to occur. The PETT promoted privatization as the means to solve the endemic lack of titles in Peru. According to the Ministry itself, however, "under current law, the titling of the communities can take two modalities: communal or individual" (PTRT 2001, 4). Yet the PETT provided no means to obtain comunidad titles. Rather, in its own literature and according to its personnel at the Ayacucho office, the PETT saw privatization as just another developmentalist resource inherently positive to all farmers. So fighting this resource was a highly illogical, self-sabotaging action. Intentionally or not, the PETT therein revived the old racism that constructs indigenous interests as irrational. In effect, the PETT was saying—was institutionally structured such that: Indians cannot understand their own best interests so must have their enlightened superiors speak for them. While this situation in and of itself insinuates the need for coercive tactics to force what is best upon the resisting native populations, the legislation bolstered this coercive tendency by not providing any real means to convince villagers that privatization was in their best interests.

In all, by refusing to help resolve local land conflicts, the policy pushed the elite to quell local discontent. Failing to provide a convincing ideological rationale, the law drove elites to coercive means. The hands-off approach meant that elites would have to present villages in the highly racially caricatured way envisioned by the PETT: as isolated, homogenous, democratic, and free of intimidation. But granting carte blanche to elites also held out race as a way to achieve this. To impose an unpopular and radical remaking of local society meant successfully representing villagers not according to what they wanted but as too ignorant to understand their best interests. But villagers fought against this.

COMUNIDAD RESISTANCE

Pedro, the same man who had risen to local prominence through his unwavering dedication to the Evangelical church, led the pro-comunidad resistance. In many ways, Pedro was an unlikely opposition leader. He only had a second grade education, though he had learned a great deal about reading and writing through his church activities, particularly reading and interpreting the Bible. This meant, for instance, that he did not understand the clause in the Land Law that said villages must decide to privatize through a two-thirds majority and instead kept stating privatization required "half plus one" ("la mitad más uno"). He spoke a heavily accented and broken Spanish and he could still present a gruff and un-open presence.

But his new leadership roles acquired via his ascendency through the church made him the default resistance leader. In this, Pedro regularly said, "I will never hate Damian; you know why? Because he showed me how to enter all the offices," meaning Damian had trained him in the difficult and highly mestizo skills of gaining resources for the village. Indeed, Pedro proved much more talented at this than any other villager with poor educations, including the cabecilla members. Thus, Pedro had close personal ties to the cabecilla and a poor education, disinclining him to lead the privatization opposition. On the other hand, his work with the church had given him the motivation and abilities to lead with what he regarded as fairness. He believed that most villagers truly wanted to preserve the comunidad and that doing so was in their best interests.

This group's strategy consisted of (1) rectifying the comunidad legal documents, (2) bringing in experts on the topic so villagers could make an informed decision, and (3) setting up a regularized, intimidation-free, formal vote on the issue so it could be decided once and for all. In this first strategy, the group sought to normalize their community documents in the relevant Ayacucho institutions. The privatizers had brought into question whether the comunidad had ever, during its previous twenty years of existence, actually been properly registered at all. To rectify this issue, the comunidad group, as they became called, tried to raise money locally, through selling a stand of eucalyptus trees, to pay for all the necessary legal services and documentation. Part of this approach included notarizing testimonials about the existence of the community, a strategy recommended by CEDAP and later overtaken by the privatizers.

The effort to regularize documentation was stillborn, inciting the then community president who was in charge of this project to threaten to resign since he seemed to lack the backing of the populace. The pro-community side blamed the privatizers for stopping this regularization. Completely regularizing community documents, however, would be a monumental if not impossible task given the sketchy nature of both documentation and urban oversight institutions. This was, of course, typical of the Andes. Herein securing a legitimate village vote on the issue acquired the utmost importance.

The second strategy consisted of bringing urban institutions to the village to explain the advantages and disadvantages of privatization and have people make informed decisions. Pedro explained that "in the Bible it says that a person has five senses and we have to use them to make whatever decision." From speaking with multiple different organizations, Pedro understood privatization as meaning the loss of land for the poor, but increased land concentration for people with larger holdings, just as the Ministry of Agriculture explained the process in their propaganda. In contrast, comunidad meant the protection of lands. Thus, he believed that villagers, if they could clearly understand privatization, would have no part in this new land tenure system.

In this spirit, then, Pedro sought help from urban institutions who could explain the advantages and disadvantages of privatization to the population. CEDAP, the Ayacucho-based non-governmental organization with long-standing connections to Huaytabamba, agreed to help, as did the Defensoría del Pueblo—the governmental human rights organization. Additionally, the district governor, the district mayor, and the Peasant Confederation of Peru (CCP) all pledged their help. All of these parties similarly supposed that community members would not voluntarily remove community protections if they sufficiently understood the implications of privatization. They likewise all stressed that village-level institutions had full responsibility for administering the vote because any help from regulating agencies would infringe on local self-determination. But they saw privatization as so counter to peasants' interests that any vote was a foregone, pro-comunidad conclusion.

Thus the comunidad side plotted to call a general meeting in which the issue would be put to a final vote, people deciding based solely on informed positions, and the enlightened democratic conclusion would be sanctified in law through passing a formal community resolution and registering the result with all the appropriate government authorities. From September 2002 through March 2003, three different organizations made similar presentations to the community in order to clear up the issue of privatization. With the opposing sides unfurling their polarized strategies, the privatization battle began.

NOTES

1. Given the high level of job seeking through various forms of migration, this rule requires some flexibility.

2. See also Vargas Llosa's 1990 article revamping this racism.

SIX

The Privatization Battle

Here then was the tableau for the coming struggle. Privatization promised a radical remaking of the community. Villagers felt deeply threatened and were fighting back. The comunidad faction had their local ethnic resources from the Evangelically revived village and anti-privatization urban allies. Meanwhile, the city-dwelling faction began mobilizing for privatization. Through bringing a rent-based economy, privatization would reorient the village to directly serve these urbanites who had been limited in their powers by comunidad regulations. Political and economic power would not only shift to the city, but would become much more privatized within urban households. The rationalities of individual urban families would drive reality in the village. Village residents, in contrast, would become servants to this rationality, reconfigured as powerless and dependent Indians supplicating distant landlords, unable to act on their own village-based interests. In other words, the racial regime would change from color-blind hegemonic exploitation to an overt sovereign form of enlightened European masters commanding powerless and ignorant Indians. And the PETT-implemented legislation already effectively treated these two factions in line with the new racial paradigm.

Under these conditions, how did the privatizers mobilize their lie about the nature of privatization? They put the cart before the horse. Instead of getting the racial results through the new political economy, they fought for privatization by racializing the villagers, by making them unable to act on their own interests through undercutting their resources. Being unable to act on their own interests, they would have no choice but to acquiesce to the urban-centric regime and act according to its logics. Thus in their integration into the neoliberal economy, being unable to act would amount to being unable to know their best interests. Helped considerably by the extant urban racialization of villagers, the privatizers worked simultaneously on several fronts: alienating villagers from the city, undermining comunidad access to urban economic resources, undercutting village-based resources, and severing comunidad alliances with urban allies.

ALIENATING VILLAGERS FROM THE CITY

"Because I am the owner of the community."
—Damian (facetiously?) explaining why he had the only full records of the original 1964 sale of lands to the villagers

As a major tactic, the privatizers insisted that all discussion had to go through the written record of the village. As Damian, shaking a dog-eared stack of papers, intoned at one meeting: "papers speak, because with the mouth sometimes we exaggerate." When I spoke to workers at the PETT, they dismissed this as incredibly unrealistic given the near absence of clear titles in the Andes.

By stressing documentation, the privatizers tried to move the debate out of the village and to the urban organizations. To the degree that the debate centered on what the documents reported, the village had no direct say over privatizing. Instead of debating the value of comunidad versus privatization, the debate would shift to how solidly the institution of the comunidad existed in the extant records. This strategy therein pulled the issue away from local autonomy, de-politicizing it. Instead, the issue turned on technical issues. And in this way the privatizers further racialized the debate, giving advantages to the few individuals with more sophisticated levels of urban savvy. This was especially true due to the nature of land registration in rural Peru and its high susceptibility to manipulation and conflict.

More specifically, the privatizers used the scarcity of documentation to insist that the comunidad as a legitimate political institution did not exist. As Damian explained to me: "they want to maintain the comunidad but they lack documents." But the privatizers spelled this out as part of a hugely complex and difficult to understand system. As Damian narrated the lack of comunidad documentation at one meeting:

> This record of a search for the property title of the Peasant Community of Huaytabamba, that this says is negative. A notice of search for the document of sale of the hacienda Huaytabamba in the name of Héctor AV, Dolores GB, that is negative. A copy of the formula certificate of tax payments to the Ministry of Haciendas and Commerce National Superintendent of Contributions and Registry of the Contributions of Taxes to the Rent of Mobile Capital; and they said that the Peasant Comunidad of Huaytabamba does not appear at the PETT, that is the Special Project for the Titling of Lands.

Guillermo Nugent (2005) finds the waving of these "paper flags" a long-standing tradition in the Peruvian congress that enables the triumph of fundamentalism over redistributive justice. In the countryside, such manipulation through an insistence on sticking with the sparse extant documentation is a major facet of *tinteriaje* or "playing the role of the lawyer." The guise of legality and most people's alienation from the judiciary provides brokers a powerful instrument to manipulate the system (Poole 2004). Even in the rare instances when intermediaries resolve their conflicted position in favor of rural areas, they remain highly paternalistic, with brokers not teaching their skills to their wards but rather operating on their behalf and preserving this tool for themselves. The stark contrast between the incredibly sketchy existing legal record and the adamancy with which tinterios insist on hewing to the record shows the inherent manipulation of this process.

In Huaytabamba this became ever clearer as the documentation-insisting privatizers simultaneously worked to undermine the records of the village that they did not like, such as by spiriting away most of the archive of community meetings. Ironically, the brokers had written most of these records themselves. But this was under the very different conditions of ruling through the community rather than against it. The records indicate, for instance, that the comunidad general assemblies empowered the brokers to act on behalf of the village and with urban organizations such as DICCPUM (see chapter 3). Gaining authority through the comunidad meant that the privatizers had earlier acknowledged the legitimacy of the comunidad as a legal and empowered entity. Now, though, it stood in their way of realizing their privatization designs so such documentation was problematic.

Bringing this tradition to the Huaytabamba privatization struggle, Damian's explanation was deliberately deceptive in both form and content. As to form, Damian was portraying urban institutions as (1) inaccessible for their complexity, and (2) dangerous for their duplicity in constructing the legal framework of the village as not reflecting the experiences of the villagers themselves. As such, this helped the privatizers craft and assert their inverted understanding of privatization. Content-wise, this description did not reflect the general realities of these institutions nor how they engaged with the privatization issue. PETT would not have any records of the comunidad, for instance, because that was not their function. Further, Damian never mentioned the public registry where documentation did exist.

In speaking about the entirety of the village's archive, upon which he claimed the future depended, Damian was similarly devious. His overall point was that no coherent record documenting the village as a comunidad currently existed so that actions based on this framework, such as voting whether to privatize, were not legitimate. Aside from the fact that the PETT, the public registry, and other urban organizations disagreed with this assessment, Damian himself was self-admittedly at the center of this lack of documentation.

Damian, it turned out, had a godfather at the Ministry of Agriculture. When Huaytabamba had its 1980s land dispute with the neighboring village, Damian convinced this man to give him the documents, which by law had to stay at the Ministry, so that the village could make a winning case to the judge. Damian maintains that these documents were left in a restaurant that subsequently burned down. Though he admits that the documents existed at one time, he asserts that the lack of the documents left the comunidad null and void. Of course, the real issue was not about documentation at all. PETT and other government agencies recognized the village as a comunidad. Damian was merely using the lack of documentation as a ruse to intimidate villagers into accepting privatization as the only option.

The privatizers bolstered this point by claiming that the village had never actually been officially registered as a comunidad. Instead, they argued that the village had simply gone through some of the motions with an official in the agency who had a connection to the former hacendado of the land who was granting them favors because of their special social relations. Damain explained that the official came to the village and the official and villagers sanctified their relationship through making several *panchamancas* (earth oven meals). In this way, they could get access to programs earmarked for comunidades, but they would not have to strictly abide by the rules about land transfers and village participation.

When I showed Damian a copy of the registration of the comunidad I had obtained through the public registry, he prevaricated, making obscure claims about the out-of-date laws upon which this registration was based and that other documents were needed to actually prove registration. The registry personnel scoffed at such a claim.

The privatizers thus began to try and manipulate the urban records of the village. In one major gambit, the privatizers notarized testimonials from the patriarchs in which they claimed that the comunidad structure never really existed. Instead, they maintained that a private property regime had persisted since villagers initially purchased the lands from the hacienda owner in the 1960s. On these testimonials they listed all the original purchasers—many of them deceased—and submitted this documentation to the public registry to have the state sanctify the village as private and not a comunidad. The public registry, however, explained that dead people cannot own lands. They similarly engaged with the Ministry of Agriculture and the PETT, the latter telling them it would be much easier to privatize with the cooperation of the entire village.

The privatizers said that their work to rectify local records would only serve individuals who signed up for privatization. And this new documentation would lock the people without documentation—the vast majority—into a path of imminent land loss. They told villagers, both in public meetings and through regular visits to their homes: "if you are not in this privatization you are going to lose your fields."

This working behind the scenes, shuttling back and forth between the village and the city offices, proved an important tool of intimidation. As one villager lamented: "When Damian was in another place everything was fine; and now that he has returned he has put us in problems and says that the paperwork [for privatization] is accelerating." After each different urban visit, the privatizers returned to the village saying the paperwork is almost complete. Most villagers began to feel fearful and uncertain about the entire situation, a condition exacerbated by other parallel broker actions.

In total, this part of the privatization strategy worked through simultaneously insisting on the authority of the city over privatization and increasing villagers' alienation from these same institutions. The brokers leveraged their privileged cultural capital not in order to control lucrative development projects as occurred previously, but to increase their authority over the interpretation and implementation of the new legislation. While the comunidad faction may not necessarily have believed these statements, as noted above, they partially acquiesced to it by believing the issue of village records played a determinant role. They thereby undermined their own comunidad case by granting the privatizers greater authority over the issue and eroded the authority of their own case that a free and fair village vote should decide the question.

CUTTING URBAN SOCIOECONOMIC SUPPORT

While the privatizers attempted to shift the terms of the debate, they also employed their privileged positions in a new and largely inverted way to serve their neoliberal purposes. Rather than bolstering the village through providing development resources and therein securing their authority, the brokers now sought to undermine the viability of the comunidad through weakening its key practices. In this, the brokers continued to represent the village and therein embody comunidad self-determination. The privatizers realized some of the easiest and farthest-reaching successes here. And in this, they provided real substance to their threats, forcefully demonstrating that they could bring about the conditions that they claimed would occur through adhering to the comunidad system.

With varying degrees of success, the privatizers targeted the three major aspects of the comunidad that supported the daily strategies of the villagers: development projects, mutual aid, and the office of the comunidad president. External development projects proved one of the easiest targets. The brokers employed the same privileges they had used to extort moneys through projects. Now, though, they used these to prevent projects from entering the village. Foremost, because urban agencies still adhered to the solicitor model, they granted intermediaries near full power in these decisions, though most agencies still adhered to developmentalism and assumed that villages desired whatever project came their way. In this way, Huaytabamba lost out on a new school, a grinding mill, a reconstructed community potato storage barn, a road up to the pastures, and several other projects.

For their part, the privatizers explained to me: "the future of the comunidad is uncertain; we cannot have projects with such uncertainty." On its surface, this may seem to make some sense, needing stable institutions to govern external funds and initiatives. But this was actually a inversion of the relationship between projects and the village, therein revealing the true strategic nature of this action. Rather than needing the comunidad to run the projects, villagers desired the institution of the comunidad because it helped them coordinate their outsized collective desire for any and all external programs. Furthermore, the comunidad does not manage the programs. Single intermediaries work in conjunction with urban officials to make sure projects adhere to the goals of the sponsoring agencies.

Rather, as the director of CEDAP put it, "We cannot enter until they solve this problem," because any investment ran the serious risk of being siphoned off by the opportunistic privatizers, just as previous moneys had been misappropriated. The pervasiveness of the institutionalized segregation of the village therein demonstrates itself as even organizations desiring to help the comunidad felt at mercy to the impunity of the brokers.

The privatizers therein used their racially enabled brokerage positions to undermine this key facet of community life, while demonstrating their abilities to dictate key village policies, and threatening villagers. Villagers lost economic resources but also lost some faith in the viability of the comunidad. And truncating project delivery eroded the social networks through which the comunidad faction could make urban connections. All told, the comunidad faction lost an ideological battle about the validity of the comunidad. They also lost a political battle about who could exercise control in the village. And the privatizers began reforming the nature of brokerage.

UNDERMINING VILLAGERS FROM WITHIN

Concurrent with external programs, the privatizers also attacked the local practices of mutual labor exchange: the village-wide faena and the personal ayni. In many ways, these represented the ethnic backbone of the community, expressing and working for mutual interests. The privatizers stopped participating in these reciprocal labor exchanges, contested the traditional calling of faenas by the comunidad president, and encouraged others to halt their participation, asserting that the pro-comunidad faction would usurp the fruit of these efforts. As one president of the comunidad lamented, "the elders no longer participate in the faenas; they only make trouble." At first, faenas continued, with the privatizers free-riding off the labor of the rest. But both the faena and ayni eventually came to a halt once privatization became a daily facet of village life. As conflict escalated, working together proved largely untenable.

This demonstrates brokers employing their localized ethnic powers, the outsized status they enjoyed in the village enabling a small group to eventually erode the viability of long-standing and much desired comunidad practices. But their ethnic status also drew from other resources. As the most wealthy village members, their class standings enabled them to hire many more people as part of the ayni system and provide people with rare opportunities to earn cash locally, so their withdrawal dramatically cut the ability to regularly marshal sizeable labor groups and make the ayni a regular practice. Their ethnic status also importantly came from their racial privileges of being able to uniquely deal with urban agencies and bring projects to the village.

As has been documented in other cases, the deliberate violation of these norms amounts to a show of power and enforcement of local hierarchy (cf. Gose 1994). Displaying an acute understanding of local ethnic mores and deliberately violating them sets elites above such practices that they racially deride as Indian. In this instance, though, the more deliberate acts—particularly arguing against the traditional calling of faenas for village maintenance reasons—went further. Instead of eroding faena effectiveness through freeloading, local leaders began garnering their power from undercutting the entire ethnic institution. This was, in effect, a privatization of ethnic work parties and other key village functions. Instead of mutually recognized developmentalist needs, such functions would only occur through the whims—and to serve the interests—of local power holders. Urban agencies were implicated in this as well, though. External projects work through faenas, with outside funding making these practices their most robust. Acquiescing to broker demands to cut local projects therein bolstered brokers' abilities to undercut faenas and thus the comunidad.

Through these actions the privatizers also attacked the office of the comunidad president, rendering even its smallest functions untenable. For instance, partially acquiescing to the privatizers' argument that the village's fate depended on extant paperwork, the president at the time, don Wilfredo, attempted to raise money from villagers to rectify the archive in the Ministry of Agriculture. Unable to gain funds, Wilfredo resigned (temporarily), viewing this as a vote of no confidence. The presidency similarly could not serve other regular functions, with the position increasingly hanging on resolving the privatization issue. People no longer sought the president to solve localized disputes, such as cows impinging into fields. And the major function of acquiring external resources was totally undermined. Thus, all local issues became increasingly folded into the polarized privatization debate, the resolution of which would decide the fates of almost every other aspect of village life.

The privatizers similarly attacked the comunidad faction, simultaneously undermining its capacity to mount resistance while demonstrating the extent of broker power. In one major instance, Damian crafted a libelous letter to the district governor, denouncing Pedro, the leader of the pro-comunidad faction and also the village-elected governor's representative. The letter never mentioned privatization, and utilized a tangle of legalese to assert its point. Content-wise, Damian blamed his rival for the reality that Damian himself created:

> We consider that this man is usurping the functions of the comunidad authorities, interfering in what he should not, creating discord, incomprehension between the *comuneros* [comunidad members], including dividing the comuneros in two (2) groups, with he and his allies taking whatever resources come from non-governmental entities.

The letter complained that Pedro was deliberately fracturing the village in order to consolidate political and economic power. It goes on to paint this one man as a tyrant imposing his will on the village majority and as stripping protections from the older residents. Moreover, it claims that Pedro is not even a legitimate community member (*no calificado*), so he lacks any legal authority. He is an outsider "interfering in the smooth running [*buena marcha*] of the community."

In contrast, the complainants assert their authority as based on both Western legal traditions ("according to Arts. 1 and 2 of the General Law of Peasant Communities No 24656") and local ethnic autonomy, through the practices of

> communal work and using the land . . . ancestral, social, economic, and cultural links . . . equality of rights and obligations . . . defense of the common interest, clear participation in institutional life, solidarity, reciprocity and mutual help.

In the end, this letter failed to remove Pedro from office or the comunidad. But, this letter epitomizes the new privatization strategy, its fearless use of fraud, and its endless impunity. The letter displays the privatizers' unique facility with urban agencies. The filing of the letter shows the brokers employing their cultural capital to attack their opponents. It demonstrates the privatizers' savvy with grasping the kind of language potable to urban institutions. The letter panders to agencies' racialized understandings of comunidades, as authentic redoubts of ethnic harmony beset by manipulative outsiders. The letter thus shows the privatizers' willingness to represent the village in the racist way that agencies, particularly the PETT, need so as to allow privatization. The fact that Damian abused the system without getting punished demonstrates the great leeway the privatizers enjoyed in attempting to realize their desires. And finally, the brazen fraud perpetrated by the letter shows the great lengths the privatizers will go to realize their goals.

SEVERING POLITICAL SUPPORT

The privatizers also exacerbated the racialized relations between village and city in order to cut the comunidad faction from urban allies. After failing to call a vote following each of the presentations on the Land Law, the pro-comunidad faction attempted to bring the various officials who had promised help to come and actually regulate the decision making process. These included the mayor, judge, and governor from the district, as well as CEDAP and the Defensoría. Against this threat, the privatizers launched a vicious campaign condemning such actions as external manipulation and undermining community sovereignty. That this autonomy was based on the comunidad government, the specific entity the privatizers sought to bring down, was apparently not an important point for the privatizers—again displaying their breadth of power and willingness to stoop to whatever duplicitous means they could.

The actions against the district mayor were particularly vicious, making malicious statements but also playing on his own racializing tendencies. The privatizers denounced the mayor, including through the Quechua language radio station, for soliciting votes through building the new primary school in Huaytabamba that remained filled with stagnant water and never saw any pupils (see chapter 3). As one extension worker put it, "the mayor got them all to vote for him and now this school is flooded." The privatizers condemned the mayor, saying, "this is not a school; this is only a corral; you who have been a teacher and now are mayor should fix it." While the school construction was clearly corrupt, what the privatizers conveniently overlooked was that the project was brokered locally by one of their own who actually gained a seat in the mayor's administration for doing so. Further, such corruption constitutes the normal quid-quo-pro behavior of rural Peru.

Really, what the privatizers were doing was defending the territory where they dictated local laws. Given the mayor's exalted position, he was particularly vulnerable to his corruption coming to light. The mayor, though, had a racialized out. He rebuffed the privatizers saying, "this was not a work of the mayor's office but a work of the community itself." In other words, because the system of resource procurement lacked meaningful accountability, the mayor could dismiss his corrupt behavior as an internal community issue. The institutions were set up to enable the mayor to blame the victims. But by abdicating his authority over such local projects he also undermined his authority to help regularize the

Huaytabamba privatization vote. Damian regularly operated through such means, readily condemning his peers—including his privatization allies—for their corruption while blaming his own corrupt projects on the inability or ignorance of the villagers.

The mayor, like the other officials, did not expect such brazen hostility, but rather thought their roles would be more formal and based on their authority. Thus, when they were blindsided, they quickly pulled back from their promises. On the day Pedro had scheduled external authorities to come help regulate a final vote on the matter, he and I scoured the provincial capital to get the mayor and the judge to make good on their promises. But they had clearly quit the field and could not be found. The privatizers provided the convenient racialized back door of dismissing village problems as internal pathologies unrelated to the larger world. After all, these urban authorities had no institutional or legal obligation to fulfill a regulatory role and they gladly fell back on this lest the accusations of manipulation stick on them and ruin their careers. Of course, this is the point: indigenous people are largely racialized through institutions maintaining double standards. And the officials retreating to these standards meant they helped perpetuate Huaytabamba racialization simply through doing their jobs.

Overall, the privatizers had a much easier time keeping urban agencies from regularizing the privatization process than they had convincing villagers of privatization's benefits. The privatizers had to engage in some aggressive actions to remove their urban competition. But mostly they could rely on their opponents' own vulnerability to corruption charges while offering them the easy out of continuing their racialized isolation of the villagers.

THE FALL OF THE CHURCH

The hostility of the struggle eventually took a toll on all village practices, making them conflict-ridden to the point of not functioning. Most tellingly, the Evangelical church—through which the village had previously revitalized itself—experienced rapid decline. While generally perceived as a place of retreat and fellowship amidst an uncertain world, privatization eventually entered the pews and tore the church apart until only the pastor and his wife attended.

The privatizers attacked it, Damian's father, for example, declaring that "don Pedro dresses and eats with the offerings and contributions that we give [through the Evangelical church] and now no longer farms." And such a polarized debate drove the devoutly faithful from each other and their beloved church. For example, one of Damian's brothers, who was almost elected pastor himself and was ambivalent about privatization, explained that during services "sometimes they say bad things about my family, about my brother [Damian] and my father; this hurts me and for this I do not participate in the church." Yet this same man was similarly accused by his uncle: "my nephew is in privatization and says bad things [at church] because we don't participate in privatization; and for this I prefer to be at peace and by myself praying at home." Instead of brotherhood keeping the flock together, misunderstanding and disregard splintered it.

More than just itself, though, the fall of the church demonstrated the success with which the privatizers had sundered the comunidad. The church had revitalized the comunidad in a way that resolved intermediaries' dilemma in favor of the village. Even more, though, unlike the inherent political nature of most other village practices, the church deliberately had non-political aspects, despite the fact that Pedro had politicized some facets. Thus, the penetration of the divisive politics of privatization into the church signaled a broad deterioration of the entire community.

RACISM CONQUERS DEMOCRACY

The comunidad faction repeatedly tried to call the matter to a final vote and end the conflict. This plan never reached fruition, however, because the racialized isolation of the village made a free and fair vote impossible. The community faction secured village presentations from three different organizations believing that a village vote would immediately follow based on the information provided. For instance, when Pedro and I visited the Defensoría del Pueblo, the government-sponsored human rights ombudsman, the young lawyer working there explained the law in easy terms and said he would have no problem making a presentation to the village. Before this, CEDAP had made a similar presentation. Both of these organizations saw privatization as against the best interests of the villagers. But they also believed that the community should make their own decision. Both organizations expected that the village authorities could successfully call a community meeting to hear the presentation and vote immediately and finally on the issue.

Herein these pro-community organizations make grievous assumptions that unwittingly make them participate in the racialization of the villagers. First, in their handling of the privatization issue, the organizations do not recognize the informal and manipulation-prone environment governing rural Peru. Tellingly, these organizations, while critical of the Land Law, still spoke of it as a mechanical instrument. They failed to elucidate that, while the law allows for either a private or a community option, it does not specify any process through which to regulate this decision. Any purported expert should have easily recognized that the law as written suffers from a terrible vagueness making it particularly prone to manipulation, and should have suggested making arrangements to make the local process as transparent and free from intimidation as possible.

The behavior of the Defensoría lawyer during his presentation is instructive on this point. Getting to the village involves an hour-long bus ride and a forty-five minute walk. This man happily made the journey but refused all succor when he finally arrived. And village cultural norms highly stress that all visitors should receive food and drinks upon arrival. He clearly strove to achieve a professional distance from all villagers so his information would come across as simply informative and unbiased. Such behavior, however, denied the manipulative informality dominating political processes. Rather, it presupposed the existence of local mechanisms to guarantee a free and open vote, even though he was also quite aware of much of the gross intimidation happening in the village. While he did not want to give the impression of manipulating the process, he did nothing to actually moderate the rampant coercion, thereby countenancing it through inaction.

To immediately counter the Defensoría presentation, the privatizers called a faena for the first time in several months. Up to this point, the privatizers had been boycotting faenas in an effort to undermine the community. Now, especially since they had cajoled a number of villagers into joining their ranks, the privatizers began employing the popular aspects of the community to serve their own purposes. The ploy was a fairly naked attempt to prevent people from hearing the Defensoría presentation. But, since almost everyone desired the preservation of faena and was upset by its deterioration, people were reluctant to contribute to its demise by not participating. More poignantly, though, one pro-community man who participated in the privatizers' faena said to me, "I know we will lose faena; I just want to work it while we still have it." In this context, he was also communicating that he knew that no decision would be made at the Defensoría meeting so the best use of his time was to directly support a major aspect of community that he cherished.

So both CEDAP and the Defensoría participated in the racialization of the village through allowing the process to be manipulated. Perhaps more crucially, however, these organizations deliberately quit the village after their presentations. True to his professionalism, the Defensoría lawyer believed he had no further role and that the authorities who invited him would now conduct a final vote on the merit of privatization and put the issue to rest based on the unbiased information he had presented. Any continued presence, he and the CEDAP officials believed, would infringe on the autonomy of the community.

Pedro's largest attempt to regularize the vote envisioned bringing in a variety of groups. As noted above, the privatizers successfully kept the district Mayor and Judge from attending. But the above organizations, the comunidad's greatest allies, refused to help. They demurred not because of threats from the privatizers, but rather because they mistakenly saw helping to bring about an intimidation-free vote as interfering with local self-determination. So they declined offers to help regulate a vote because they thought they were respecting village autonomy. In stark contrast to the village's potential vote, the highly contested 2000 national elections witnessed multiple international groups attempting to monitor and maintain the process as transparent, free, and fair. This gross double standard is only applied to peasant communities and explicitly in the name of their autonomy. In all other circumstances, the dominant culture views clear and coherent regulation as the only way to guarantee the triumph of the popular will, while complaints of external interference are regarded as manipulative tools of corrupt tyrants.

The inability of the village to host an orderly vote on the matter illustrates the extreme barriers created by their racialized incorporation into society. It also shows how such incorporation results in the racialized outcomes of fully lacking due process and instead having people with opposed interests represent them. The Land Law created the two-thirds clause, however paternalistically, to safeguard indigenous interests. Yet villagers were ultimately unable to exercise this right. The PETT provided no means to do so—let alone exercise the right to a clear comunidad-based title. Local officials, the best-placed people to do the job, did not want to regulate lest they put themselves in the middle of an acrimonious conflict. Since it was not required of them, they eagerly retreated. And the villagers' greatest allies refused to help simply because they held on to mistaken and ultimately racist beliefs that helping to regularize village-level votes infringed on self-determination when in fact the opposite was true. With no external aid, the villagers could never get their desires codified into law. In the end, attempts at a democratic decision-making process fell in front of the racialized incorporation of villages.

COUP D'ETAT, COUP DE GRÂCE

Throughout this time, various villagers switched to the private side under the constant pressure. I questioned one man who generally regarded the privatizers contemptuously: "I just want this [conflict] to end; I want to return to the way we were [meaning without conflict]. . . . I have no papers for my fields; I cannot lose my fields." Previously he expressed to me that while he knew no real specifics of the privatization issue, he regarded the privatizers as jerks full of bluff and bluster though with no real threat. He said he had earlier considered privatization because the cabecilla had personally appealed to him. But he resented Damian's contemptuous manipulation. He had said that Damian deserved death for his previous fleecing of village resources. But now he could not tolerate the constant pressure. He said he did not know if the privatizers could take his fields. It had reached the point for him, however, that he no longer wished to risk it. Soon after, he and others like him ended up working in the privatizers' fields, allegedly to work off the costs of the privatization process.

In February 2003, however, the privatizers made a bold move and established their own competing village government replete with the regalia of a notarized book of minutes and stamps for all the officers. With this move, the privatizers literally divided the village in two. Urban officials consulted by the pro-comunidad faction dismissed this act as fraudulent and illegal. Yet no mechanism existed for the comunidad group to successfully challenge the legitimacy of the private government. In and of itself, the establishment of a parallel government did not immediately break the comunidad, but it seriously consolidated the privatizers' legitimacy and authority.

With this government, the privatizers began to put themselves in direct control over village resources, and to use them towards their privatization ends. In one of the most threatening moves to villagers, the privatizers started liquidating comunidad resources. The funds, they said, would go towards financing the privatization effort. But this move demonstrated to the villagers that if they were not on the privatization side, they would lose out on their share of the comunidad resources. As one privatizer explained: "To those who don't inscribe [into privatization] we are not going to give; to those of us in the private property we are going to redistribute" the proceeds. In other words, the privatizers sought to sell village resources and use the proceeds as a bribe for those who acquiesce and a threat to those who resist.

In March of 2003, the privatizers declared that they were going to sell the stand of eucalyptus trees above the village. This was a major source of material for both cooking and construction. The privatizers' sales incited a panic in the population and the villagers grabbed the wood in a nearly free-for-all manner. This resulted in deforestation, with scars opening up on the steep hillside where inhabitants dragged their logs. The gouged hillsides threatened flooding and massive erosion when the rains returned in the winter. This deforestation coincided with the visit of the general secretary of the Peruvian Peasant Confederation (CCP) who came to deliver the third explanation of the privatization process. While previous presentations had occurred in the main square with most villagers in attendance, this last one occurred in the yard of a house attended by a very few subdued villagers. While the CCP presentation unequivocally denounced privatization, his words did little to calm the panicked villagers who were watching resources flow rapidly out of comunidad hands. The openly anti-privatization numbers had dwindled precariously.

Indeed, this show of power finally demonstrated to people that the privatizers were not bluffing in their claims and that people would indeed lose out in their access to land if they did not acquiesce. Additionally, it provided the privatizers large amounts of funding with which to further their efforts. In addition to the eucalyptus, the private government broke up and sold off the comunidad stockade, and threatened to eventually do the same to the large comunidad fields and pastures.

Later that same month, the privatizers presented legal documents supporting their case. They unearthed a document from the public registry, dated July 1998, that showed the initial purchasers of land in the 1960s, many of them dead or out-migrated, as the current legal landholders. The privatizers used this document to further insist that people who purchased subsequently—the vast majority of current inhabitants—lacked legal possession of their land.

Damian explained the origin of the document. When the cabecilla initially attempted to privatize the land in 1998, they followed the Ministry of Agriculture's advice and made a legal claim that the village lands were held as private property. Though the claim was never substantiated, the patriarchs published the claim. According to Damian, because the claim was never revoked or contested, the claim stood as the legal record of the village:

> In 1998, the public registry had published it. In the newspapers and everything they had published it, allowing people to say it was a Peasant Community, so they could block it. They have not blocked it, nobody has said, "you know, this is a comunidad, this is not private property"; they have not done it. . . . They should have blocked it, Pedro and all the others, "no sirs, this is already a comunidad, this should be annulled." And they did not annul it. It stays being private property.

This was an age-old story of a dispossession process: filing supposedly public papers that the victims had no actual means to access.[1] As the Ministry and the privatizers well knew, there was almost no way that anybody in the village could have been aware of this claim or the legal process in general.

This document, and its emergence at the time that the privatizers were seizing village control, served as a final punctuation to the privatization struggle. This was the fraudulent yet legalistic guise that the privatizers employed to justify their usurpation of village authority. The document's origins, with its gross manipulation through the direct assistance of urban agencies, reflected the alienation and disenfranchisement of villagers in their situation of institutionalized segregation. This paper represented the village and villagers opposite from their actual desires and experiences. Its timely presentation echoed the process of villager acquiescence. Damian presented it as proof of the correctness of the privatizers' analysis, particularly of the imminence of land loss. The public registry personnel scoffed at it saying: "how can dead people own lands?" The villagers, however, did not contest it or Damian's interpretation—as a dramatic contrast to Damian's falsified petition early in the struggle. With the loss of the broad array of comunidad resources and the establishment of the private government, the fight had gone out of villagers. The legalistic framework of this document merely provided a thin veneer of legitimacy. All that remained was creating the document that would present the villagers to the PETT as freely desiring privatization.

NEOLIBERALISM AS A RITUAL OF SUBORDINATION

"The tradition of all dead generations weighs like a nightmare on the brains of the living. And just as they seem to be occupied with revolutionizing themselves and things, creating something that did not exist before, precisely in such epochs of revolutionary crisis they anxiously conjure up the spirits of the past to their service, borrowing from them names, battle slogans, and costumes in order to present this new scene in world history in time-honored disguise and borrowed language."
—Karl Marx, *The Eighteenth Brumaire*, 1852

This chapter of the fates of Huaytabamba villagers began in an Evangelically revitalized time when empathy, however weakly, ruled over exploitation. The extractive realities of Damian's previous development schemes had vanquished fantasies of vast commercial windfalls. Instead, ideas of ethnic mutuality came to enable difficult life strategies based on free access to land subsidizing below subsistence wages. More importantly, the newly stabilized local ethno-political system held potential for people to demand better circumstances, just as natives have regularly created novel resistance strategies.

Elsewhere, market fundamentalists and their "childish passion for mathematics and for purely theoretical and often highly ideological speculation" (Piketty and Goldhammer 2013, 32) dreamed of a better life for all through structural adjustment and global market integration. As neoliberalism slouched towards Huaytabamba, however, an old tradition began to weigh.[2] The spirits of the past, seemingly costumed in nineteenth-century ideas newly embroidered full of passionate intensity, actually originated from a much dimmer history.

The conquistadores lusted after gold, but realized their dreams in massive feudal estates that dwarfed their European progenitors. Their bitter dependence on native labor trapped them on their estates and into civil wars, while upon the Indian the blood-dimmed tide was loosed. Neoliberalism finally makes the conquistadores' full dream possible, a globally integrated transnational elite creating value out of financial fantasies. In this widening gyre, the center cannot hold: neoliberalism fully resolves the brokers' dilemma in favor of the urban and hoists all dependence upon the Indian. The remarkable and liberatory growth of intensive capitalism seems but a historical anomaly. Instead, the engines of extensive growth, of accumulation by dispossession, run a vibrant feu-dalism, where all things, even the incomes of the bourgeoisie themselves, depend on the godlike arbitrary patronage of the wealthy.[3] This is the second coming of the feudal lords, emancipated from land-rents into infinitely fungible debt collecting. This financial logic expels and makes expendable the general population, with whispers of the past's bloody excesses difficult to ignore.

Just as the world has come to believe that "fiendish, Frankenstein monsters of financial engineering"[4] not only hold worth but embody the cutting edge of capitalism, so the struggle in Huaytabamba amounted to imbuing symbols on paper with new meanings and therein altering the village valence. This was an ideological battle here just as anywhere. Akin to Margaret Thatcher's bold TINA statement that There Is No Alter-native—despite active and vital examples to the contrary—the privatizers won the ideological battle not through alluring appeals, but through dis-mantling the opposition, putting creativity into destruction but not gen-erating anything new.

That is, villagers never saw privatization itself as possessing inherent worth, or even came to a consensus through a hegemonic incorporation of dissent. Instead, as a poignant example of the self-actualizing process of neoliberalism, of its capacity for "making itself true" (Bourdieu 1998, 95), an acquiescence to privatization occurred once the brokerage of the privatizers—through such actions as preventing external programs, stop-ping the faena, and liquidating comunidad resources—reached the point that villagers believed the threats, and that they could actually lose their lands. What villagers thought about privatization did not matter. What mattered was what people believed Damian was capable of doing. As one anti-privatization stalwart put it:

> We finally entered [privatization] when they said that "the papers are already being rectified, they are going to come out. When all of our papers come out you all are going to be out [of the village]"; when they told us this we entered into their record book and recorded our names; now they are saying "whoever doesn't want to enter is going to remain out and is going to serve us like *cholos*."[5] They have also told us "if your fields don't have papers we are going to take these fields." For this reason we are now in this privatization, wanting to fix our papers, because on our fields' papers only the name of our seller figures and not our names.

At the beginning of this struggle, Damian held a piece of paper, openly lifted from another document that he alleged showed the consent of the majority to privatization. This quick and cheap manipulation failed large-ly because it did not meet PETT requirement for only privatizing conflict free fields, because villagers openly contested it. Since that time, Damian and his coterie successfully convinced villagers that their lands faced imminent threat, only rectifiable through privatization.

In other words, he convinced the majority that they desperately needed a piece of paper imbued with the meaning he had previously and fraudulently claimed to possess. Villagers weighed the options of immediate land loss due to the market generating process or the likely possibility of future land loss through market machinations. They chose to privatize and save their lands for the near future. The privatizers could now craft the document with which to represent the village as the PETT required: a conflict and manipulation free redoubt of democracy eager to embrace a privatized future.

Fittingly, villagers never got a final vote on privatization, even though mandated by the Land Law. Instead, privatization came through a ritual of subordination. The documents selected for the imbuing of neoliberal mestizo valence were the two tomes created to document the original sales from the hacienda that had formerly occupied the village site. While generated by an informal and unregulated process, these books stood as the founding documents of the village, and served as the sole documentation for everyone's landholdings. Along with most of the other village archives, these tomes had disappeared during the privatization struggle. With its resolution, however, Damian suddenly had them in his possession, joking, as I note above, that he should since he owned the community. Otherwise, he claimed that a village patriarch had buried them in the ground for safekeeping.

Now, the privatizers laid the books open in a dusky room in Damian's father's house just at the edge of the central plaza. In acts of obeisance, evenings saw the newly privatizing shuffle into the flickering candlelit room to hunt the original sales of the lands they now possessed. The literate, mestizo-astute sons created papers documenting the transfers from earlier owners. And one of the four cabecilla member, critical witnesses to a forged history, testified to the legitimacy, affixing their thumbprints as guarantee. To further demonstrate fealty, the privatization converts worked for free in the privatizers' fields, ostensibly to help pay for the costs of privatizing.

This ritual deeply signaled an acquiescence—rather than a consent—to a new valence of the lands. These decaying books originally stood for limited forms of self-determination and liberation from the arbitrary rule of the hacendado. And later conversion to a comunidad brought an increase in these limited powers. Reinscribing the current landholders through the thumbprint of the illiterate cabecilla, however, began reversing this process, abdicating self-determination and political decision-making to the interests of the locally powerful.

In true neoliberal fashion, Damian used this highly contentious process to depoliticize the most political issue—control of the land—and recreate it as a mere technical issue. As Aihwa Ong (2006, 3) explains, "governing activities are recast as nonpolitical and nonideological problems that need technical solutions." But as an example of the "technology of government," the lack of ideological consensus about the problem meant that submitting to the technological solution conferred a highly authoritarian kind of sovereign power. In the simplest terms, signing up for privatization did not address the largely non-existent threat of imminent land loss. Instead, it established a full new set of relations—valence—of the lands, centered on urban mestizo rent-seeking activities.

With this change, mestizos dominated less through a few individuals making deliberate acts of brokerage and much more through the majority simply operating according to their normal urban priorities. People could now fully live in the city, never fulfill any village obligation, and dedicate their lands to non-productive activities. The shift to rents meant that the high risks involved in Andean agriculture transferred from the landowners and more directly onto the villagers. And the overall risks increased because villagers had to make their agricultural activities profitable to pay rent to keep access to land that had formerly been guaranteed by the comunidad. This was a much more efficient and stable form of surplus extraction because the former means of manipulation through development projects had been replaced by simple, regular rent payments. While power shifted to the city, this enhanced broker power rather than undermining it, providing it with an institutionalized support for its continual resolution in favor of the urban.

Thus, as a result of privatizing, the villagers found themselves in a new ethnic regime that predicated villager wellbeing on fealty to the powerful over any kind of group mutuality. Indian villagers now had to realize their personhood through urban mestizos whose power no longer came from shoring up the village as under developmentalism. Their power instead flowed through economically leveraging their now fully commoditized lands, priorities centered on maximizing financial profitability rather than labor reproduction, priorities that undermined village survival strategies. In other words, with the neoliberal weakening of the exploitation cycle that tied mestizos and Indians together, highly unequal relations of personal endearment predominated, with mestizos oriented to liquidating these land-goods from which such relations arose. That is, Indians had to realize their personhood through mestizos who saw Indian interests as perverse.

Finally, these emergent social relations rendered village resources much more readily appropriable by financial capital. Their control not only became increasingly concentrated among a few individuals, but individuals whose own urban-based economic logic rested not on preserving landholdings to undergird reproductive strategies, but on the rent-seeking behavior of capitalizing on land control by *not* working the land. The lands had been rendered financial and increasingly under the control of people ready to transfer them should the right windfall opportunities arise.

Importantly, all this occurred through neoliberalism enabling a transformation of the existing racialized system to an overt racism that ideologically and institutionally incorporated natives as incapable of acting in their own best interests. The Land Law itself provided the contours for this overt racism, insisting that Indians had to have their lands taken from them for their own good—and the wellbeing of the entire society. Indians instead needed to be placed directly under their supposed superiors based on the fantastical market fundamentalist notion that the landless receive higher incomes when working for larger landholders.[6]

The lack of ideological appeal in the policy highly encouraged the local turn to overt racism, constructing villagers as too ignorant to understand the situation. The broader institutional segregation that provided villagers with no regularized means to exercise their interests instead concentrated power among the brokers, enabling them to act out this overtly racist representation of villagers. The implementation of the law specifically provided such means by (1) failing to offer the much more indigenous friendly comunidad title as specified by the law, and (2) providing no protections for villagers even while the law recognized that they needed such protections, that is by not providing a viable means to exercise the two-thirds majority clause. And the widespread ideology mistaking segregation as autonomy rationalized the inaction of external agencies, such that even the best lacked all convictions.

NOTES

1. In *The Hitchhiker's Guide to the Galaxy*, Douglas Adams has the earth destroyed through a remarkably similar process, papers properly filed—on another planet.
2. With full apologies to William Butler Yeats.
3. See Žižek (2012) for an elaboration of this important point.
4. From Paul Samuelson, another apostate neoliberal.
5. The term "cholo" has a variety of meanings in Peru. But in this instance it is used as a derisive racial slur referring to hacienda servants.
6. See Li (2011) for an insightful dismantling of such fantastical ideas.

SEVEN

The Localities and Globalities of Racism

I began this study with a historical analysis of colonial domination in Peru, in this way deriving what is central to this form of racialized rule: the reproduction of the position of conflicted intermediary that favors urban over rural interests. These figures must use their concentrated localized power for both representation and exclusion. Racial and class resources enable select individuals to assume this position. And its attendant privileges variously depend on keeping native populations ethnically fractured and therein racially subordinated. Institutionally segregated from the urban power centers, the brokers' authoritarian powers simultaneously represent the rural population's best chances for acquiring resources (broadly construed), and their greatest vulnerability to exploitation. Backed by the very real threat of blanket military reprisals, this system allows for little political dissent or negotiation, dampening discontent until it explodes. But such outbursts focus predominantly on local despots, even when they are elected officials, therein closing the circle of a system maintained by instability.

Ethnicity plays a crucial, and crucially ambiguous role in this racialized system. Ethnic relations embody the contradictory notions of (1) group mutuality and (2) allegiance to the powerful. The local "will to improve" in conditions of racially conferred privileges means that working together potentially generates better outcomes the more that power is concentrated among the much better connected elites. But this makes group members highly susceptible to exploitation, the fruit of their ethnic mutuality more easily siphoned off by elites and their need to maintain their positions through extracting local wealth. The balance between the group mutuality and elite allegiance models is frequently obscured. But it is also the main focus of the localized ethnic struggles through which the system of racial domination becomes reproduced. The resolution depends on the historical conditions, both in the type and amount of racially provided elite resources, and the ability of group members to address their institutionalized segregation.

In examining the relations of rule under developmentalism and then neoliberalism, I highlight the changing patterns of force and consent brought about through the attempted marketization of social relations, including the commodification of land, aid agencies shifting from infrastructure provision to market integration, and the undercutting of the comunidad institution as the supposed epitome of inefficiency and poverty. All these contributed to polarizing elite interests against those of the village, enabling urban-based rent collecting strategies, increasing fraud and tinteriaje, making intermediation primarily about fracturing, undermining comunidad-based bonds and practices, increasing villager alienation from urban institutions in the name of autonomy, and thus to a retrenchment of mestizo intermediaries newly empowered to favor the urban over the rural.

We can extrapolate the differences between these periods into two different regimes of racialized colonial indirect rule.[1] The first is hegemonic sovereignty, in which consent prevails over coercion. Here domination occurs through employing mestizaje to deliver development projects across the rural-urban divide, while providing villager wealth and labor to urban functionaries. Consent is acquired through a combination of an ideology of developmentalist betterment and indigenous village-level ethnic strictures against shirking. This sets off the authoritarian-exploitation cycle of successful project delivery concentrating intermediary power and increasing the flow of resources out of the village, potentially spiraling up to windfall losses.

Mestizo state developmentalism leads to exploitation based on preserving local production practices, employing rather than destroying the village level ethnically based resources acquired through the struggles culminating in the land reforms of the 1970s. Here, a color-blind form of racism delineates leadership through cumulative complex forms of self-presentation, and has these leaders represent the racialized villagers in an inclusive way that leads to their exploitation. Ethnically, group mutuality appears to predominate over loyalty to the powerful. Yet it is the strength of developmentalist ideology that obscures the relations between these two ethnic dynamics, and enables elites to harness group mutuality to the task of extraction.

Hegemony and sovereignty are frequently used as opposing forms of domination, making the concept of "hegemonic sovereignty" seemingly nonsensical. The point here, though, is that hegemonic processes of ideologically obtaining consent through developmentalist projects provided the easiest way to exercise and indeed further concentrate localized sovereign power. This was particularly true due to the village's subordination to the urban institutions that hid their exploitative activities under a veneer of hegemonic inclusiveness enabled by the brokers' sovereign power. In other words, urban institutions provided resources villagers believed they wanted (ideological hegemony) but only through a political structure that concentrated power within a single broker (sovereignty).

And indeed, this regime can only be understood through conjoining these terms. Agencies would only provide resources through a tested sovereign who proved himself and increased his power by delivering village resources to the urban organizations. And villagers had to not only submit to but largely agree that a sovereign broker was in their best interests in order to (potentially) access resources. This form of hegemony may have been thin and precarious, with villagers constantly worried about their investments—but ideological agreement still played a major role. And this involved an enormous contradiction of the hegemonic promise unfulfilled: villagers paying out ever more money and gaining less accountability. While stable, hegemony did not work without sovereignty, and sovereignty did not work without hegemony. The neoliberal turn towards marketization, however, pulled these concepts apart.

In the second type of racialized indirect rule, authoritarian sovereignty, coercion predominates over consent. Here, a much more overt form of racism predominates. The political economy cannot abide native landholdings because these undermine the ability to capture rents. Therefore natives must be incorporated both institutionally and ideologically as incapable of exercising the limited autonomy and mastery over the production process that they had enjoyed through comunidad-based access to land.

Domination occurs through dissolving rather than utilizing horizontal ethnic ties. The indigenous become more vulnerable, mestizos more powerful, and the new economic rationalities pit the interests of the two groups directly against each other, mandating a more complete dependence of the rural on the urban. Specifically, rents integrate rural production directly into the needs of urban economic rationalities. Economically, rural-based strategies become increasingly unviable as market mechanisms and the rent-based economy erodes land access.

Politically, the (non-broker) urban mestizos who had previously enjoyed little governing input because of comunidad regulations now become the primary constituency. Their economic rationalities support a governance that undermines the indigenous-associated subsistence-based strategies and attendant comunidad regulations. They instead require village-level dependence in order to insure maximal rent flows and land resource flexibility. They advocate, as simple economic rationality, the undermining of the indigenous-associated comunidad institutions, explicitly to recreate the rural Indian as a dependent that enables urban mestizo entrepreneurship. As such, indigenous dependence moves from the peripheral infrastructure under developmentalism to natives' core economic activities. Or, to put it another way, control over the production process moves from villagers following labor reproduction strategies to the landlords seeking rent maximization.

Culturally, mestizo multiculturalism—the assertion of mestizaje as legitimate difference and indigeneity as hostile, threatening, and irrational—justifies the destruction of village practices and the apotheosis of urban-based rent-seeking strategies. Mutuality all but disappears from local ethnic practices, superseded by unambiguous vertical relations wherein native wellbeing depends on fealty to capricious landlords. Thus, ideologically, mestizos are constructed as superior, having to speak for the indigenous who are too inferior to know their supposed best interests. In other words, these transformations, both in their implementation and their maintenance, normalize racist ideologies of incapable and ignorant Indians.

Finally, while the windfall exploitation involved in hegemonic sovereignty eventually undermined local leadership and the village political system, the success of authoritarian sovereignty actually enabled it to persevere despite its overt racism and engendering of increased dependency. Thus, neoliberalism brings a new form of leadership that is at once more authoritarian and more stable.

THE POLITICAL ECONOMY OF GLOBAL RACISM

Just as globalizing processes have significantly shaped the Andes and Huaytabamba in particular, the experiences of this village and its articulation with the larger society can address important issues about the changing nature of the global political economy. The starting point for this is the strange perseverance of personalism in guiding social relations, and using this to begin understanding the systemic logics that give rise to such arrangements.

The rise of industry and the bourgeoisie, "for which the discovery of America paved the way," as Marx (1848) famously tells us,

> has put an end to all feudal, patriarchal, idyllic relations. It has pitilessly torn asunder the motley feudal ties that bound man to his "natural superiors," and has left no other nexus between man and man than naked self-interest, than callous "cash payment."

He elaborates that these new arrangements must be "constantly revolutionizing" in contrast to the fact that "conservation of the old modes of production in unaltered form, was, on the contrary, the first condition of existence for all earlier industrial classes." And in this new context, people relate to each other through the things they buy: commodity fetishism. Colonialism enabled the sufficient primitive accumulation of capital to underwrite industrialization. And Marx saw market-based relations as eventually extending to the rest of the world with European colonialism breaking the back of all feudalistic relations.

As for the rentier, Marx (1844) concluded that

> the means of the extravagant rentier diminish daily in inverse proportion to the growing possibilities and temptations of pleasure. He must, therefore, either consume his capital himself, and in so doing bring about his own ruin, or become an industrial capitalist.

This analysis relies on the idea that the unique profit making forces of intensive capitalist growth will revolutionize the extensive capitalist processes of primitive accumulation.

As others have pointed out, Marx did not recognize a third possibility for the rentier: revolutionize the means of appropriation so that they can convert all manner of goods for inclusion into capitalist circuits, and thus into a means of *transferring* wealth upwards—rather than *generating* wealth and providing returns to capital.

Harvey (2003, 145) enumerates a wide range of processes through which this occurs, including slavery, imposing private property rights over all others, commodifying goods and services including labor, and arcane financial instruments. These transform a plethora of goods into a means of extraction, varying widely from basic needs such as water and food, through public services such as education and health care, to what Marx termed the common intellect or what is now called intellectual property (Žižek 2012). Thus, Harvey finds that primitive accumulation has been an ongoing process alongside capitalism, reterming it accumulation by dispossession, and shows how these conditions predominate under neoliberalism.

While not explicitly stated by Harvey, this indicates that commodity fetishism has not pervaded the world and personalism remains a key way through which people relate to one another. But what does this mean? While volumes have been written about social relations under capitalism, scholars too readily gloss over the dynamics and conundrums involved in maintaining a system that generates personalism as the key social relation. Indeed similar questions can be asked of these arrangements as with capitalism, preeminently: how do elites maintain domination? How is exploitation managed? And how is discontent controlled? In essence, what are the governing social relations that enable the perpetuation of this system? But these core questions are different under expansive capitalism in that they are asked of a situation in which no actual profit—that is, return to capital of the M-C-M' form—is gained and harnessed to these tasks. Indeed, since the industrialists have not swept away the rentiers, big questions arise about how to render rentier capitalism useful to industrial capitalism, how this relationship alters the global capitalist system, and how these are implicated in rent's rise to importance under neoliberalism.

Clearly, these questions are beyond the scope of this book. Here I simply argue that the racialization of society has played a key role in preserving the core requirements of a rentier economy. And in a relationship of circular and cumulative causality, rentiers have invested their windfall gains so as to keep racialization as the central organizing principle of society. Personalism perseveres in this dynamic because it uniquely serves the needs of both racialization and rentier economics, and as such provides the key link between the two. To grasp this, though, requires an elucidation of the relations between and dynamics of race, rentier capitalism, personalism, and feudalism.

As such, I argue that colonialism did not inadvertently—or otherwise—break the back of feudalism. Rather, the blood-soaked trial and error processes of the colonial project generated crucial means to preserve and extend feudal-type relations. Clearly, as Marx points out, the colonial process enabled the sufficient concentration of capital to underwrite European industrialization. But colonialism endeavored to make itself useful to industrial capitalism by continually supplying raw materials and absorbing the extremes of capitalist crises. In an overdetermined way, the seigniorial or aristocratic system proved preeminent for these purposes. The intertwined dynamics of racial privilege and racial marginalization enabled the perseverance of these processes. And personalism served as their lifeblood. Therefore, transformations of the global system occur through and alter the terms of racial contestation.

As has been well analyzed from a strictly class perspective, rather than a bourgeois incorporation into the global economy, colonialism mostly funneled profits from the global market to local elite groups for the purpose of control, enabling local elite to stifle internal differentiation and thus competition (Isbister 1997; Chang 2008). Colonialism, in other words, thrived through the "conservation of the old modes of production in unaltered form," actually employing the resources of global capitalism to maintain these, and quickly resorting to violence when broadly enjoyed profits on certain locally derived products threatened elite control, such as the wool boom in the Andes.

In this way, countries like Peru present a long-standing comprador bourgeoisie integrated strongly into the global economic system much more strongly than their own country (Mignolo 2000; Quijano 2000). As has been the case since conquest (Galeano 1973) these rulers struggle to capture the lion's share of rents from the extractive activities that define the economy while simultaneously trying to control the population on the cheap.

While the World Bank and their ilk can decry this group as corrupt and therein blocking of development, such disingenuous dismissals only obscure the important role that these elite play in the global economy, especially one given over increasingly to capturing rents. These leaders are corrupt in the sense that they rule through militant cronyism rather than rule of law. But this corruption is highly functional in that it has long served the needs of these elites who are mostly propped up by the global economy. Such national elite are therein not corrupt in the sense of being true to global systemic imperatives—and garnering great privileges therein.

What is missing in this analysis, however, is the racialized nature of these dynamics. The manner through which and the character of the resources racialized groups receive are set up to prevent diverse forms of integration, just as the rewards and economic rationalities of the elite groups are set up to stifle economic differentiation in order to simultaneously prevent the rise of industrial competition to the core and to keep local populations racialized.

Critical race theory powerfully argues that racialization structures racial contestation and hierarchy into the shape of social institutions, with their normal operation resulting in continued racial disparity and giving rise to ideologies justifying continued inequality. But these analyses suffer from an overly country specific focus and therefore have great difficulty in conceiving what Charles Mills (2000) terms "global white supremacy." Towards addressing this problem, I argue that the existence of racial contestation indicates the survival of an aristocratic order governed through paternalism rather than commodities and markets.

The colonial project in no way aimed towards revolutionizing the means of production. Quite the opposite, it aimed to expand and shore up feudal relations. While the Spanish Crown barely countenanced the American regicides, they looked to the New World to keep their coffers full and maintain their seigniorial rule. Similarly, the warrior class from which the conquistadores emerged ventured to the Americas explicitly to emulate their superiors and acquire large landed estates and hosts of vassals.

Herein the invention of racism proved crucial. After nearly fifty years of occupation, the colonials finally transformed the diverse native populations into Indians, a single group made fully dependent and therein organized for the purpose of exploitation. Race worked to reinscribe the feudal relations of Europe onto the Americas, establishing a rigid hierarchy between the supposedly inherently superior and enlightened white colonial lords and the misguided, helpless, heathen, and darkly complected Indian serfs. Colonials consistently used their funds to undermine economic differentiation and indigenous economic competition. Instead, they invested in keeping natives in relations of paternalist dependence—they kept natives racialized.

This is the racial legacy in coloniality. As such, since colonialism, race has worked to keep feudalistic relations a major aspect of global capitalism. In particular, racism incubates feudalism by preserving personalism, the essence of feudalism, as the defining feature of its social relations. Indeed, I would argue that paternalism is a defining feature of race (though not the other way around: paternalism can exist without racial groups). That is, the racialization of a group requires them to depend to some degree on personalistic ties, on a capricious form of resource allocation that is variously invested in preserving arbitrary authority. This is the flip side of privileged groups using social networks to preserve resources for their own members through such actions as opportunity hoarding or social closure. Rather than merit, privileged groups hoard their privileges through in-group membership.

The one form of personalism preserves privilege while the other reproduces subordination, each dependent on the other though asymmetrically. Networks of privilege depend on paternalistic subordination, but enable it through the peculiar way they provide limited resources. Paternalism requires an exceptional elite group not beholden to its peculiar logics, and enables these through its functional dysfunction.

Similarly, paternalism uniquely serves the logic of rentier economics. The rentier logics of extractive economies require (1) the ability to stifle political economic differentiation, and therefore (2) social relations based predominantly on loyalty. As we have seen, diversity in economic activities gives rise to political opposition to rentiers. But rentier economics involves other logics that help it survive. The rents captured have no direct relation to the production costs and labor expenditure. As such they can be easily captured by a small part of the population. Their disbursement thus centers not on reproducing labor and investing in the means of production but in extracting ever more materials through which to capture more rents, and undermining the kinds of economic investments and differentiation that would give rise to classes that threaten rentier control. In other words, the windfalls of rent provide rentiers with the arbitrary power to spend them, and rentiers must reproduce their position by spending their resources on stifling economic and political diversity.

While readily turning to the military to achieve these ends, paternalistic networks prove a more cost effective short-term method. Paternalism invests money to acquire loyalty, to acquire a greater number of dependents shoring up personalistic rule. Rather than having any kind of horizontal class or group interest, the logic behind the actions of these loyal subjects centers on keeping their patron in control. Merit—in the classical capitalist terms of improving the means of production—has no place because it provides the means to create rivals. Classic liberal rights–based citizenship regimes similarly contradict rentier control. These enable a wide variety of demands on national coffers and for the rule of law.

All told, racialization provided the extra-legal means to protect the rentier economics and paternalist social relations of feudalism from the revolutionary forces of the industrial bourgeoisie and other emancipatory interests emerging out of the intensification of the means of production; and the concentrated wealth and impunity provided by rentier activities supplied the means to reproduce the racialized system. While the nation-state plays a key role in this system, racialization in this context is incomprehensible without the international context. The comprador bourgeoisie explicitly and directly fought against almost any form of national self-sufficiency. Indeed, they found such ideas ideologically re-pugnant as this would make them an Indian republic. In other words, the rationalizing discourse emerging from these social relations remains un-apologetically racist, revealing the racial basis of the overall political economy.

Decades ago, Michael Burawoy (1976) asserted that racism was a par-ticular mode of incorporation into society of which powerlessness was a necessary condition. In other words, people were incorporated in such a way as to render them powerless and therein highly exploitable. While Burawoy omitted the lived experience of race, my work demonstrates that cultural practices play crucial roles in this racialized incorporation— while also providing some of the best suggestions for overcoming these relations. Adding, then, to Burawoy, I find that racist incorporation con-sists of institutionalized segregation. The institutions for the racialized generally foster and deepen dependence. Those for the dominant predi-cate relative privilege on the continued fracturing of the Other. The pater-nalism of the dominated fractures, concentrates power, and blocks eco-nomic differentiation. The paternalism of the dominant hoards resources and generates an ideology of deservingness. And the lived experiences of race play powerful naturalizing roles in these instituted relations.

Paternalism is thus a defining feature of racialization. This indicates the perseverance of some form of seigniorial rule. And such a regime requires international connections to survive, using rentier profits to ra-cially subordinate subject groups. Thus, racism is not comprehensible without understanding its integration into the global political economy. Adding paternalism and seigniorial rule to the defining features of ra-cism should thus help scholars investigate racial relations in a much wid-er terrain and better understand the racialized nature of the larger politi-cal economy. Rent-centered neoliberalism makes this ever more urgent.

With its engine of accumulation by dispossession, neoliberal policies place new emphases on colonial forms of social control, revitalizing them through lucrative elite connections to the world market. The cutting edge of today's economy demonstrates this as much as the Huaytabamba's land struggle: the masters of the universe create new and highly complex ways, such as collateralized debt obligations, to engage in primitive accu-mulation, to transfer rather than generate wealth.

The national bourgeoisie of countries like Peru face stiffening compe-tition and threat. While some enjoy huge windfalls from their special relationships with huge transnational corporations, there are fewer slots available. Moreover, foreign nationals—members of the global elite— need these corrupt intermediary figures less as they now can enjoy more direct control and less accountability through their behemoth businesses. This is a kind of corporatization of feudal relations. So both the rewards and stakes are higher. This spreads down to lower levels and into the mechanisms of indirect rule, intermediaries facing greater pressure but also more resources to resolve their brokers' dilemma almost exclusively in favor of the urban.

Towards this end, racialization in general requires more overt articulations in order to preserve its controlling features, with the funds supplied by the global economy. As many others have pointed out, marginalized groups therein face a variety of new mechanisms of control. Further, though, as Huaytabamba illustrates, these populations face layers of processes to prime them for the exclusion that integrates them into the global system. Overall, while neoliberalism spurs polarization, it also assures more crises, particularly through exacerbating the contradictions of racialized indirect rule. And crises present opportunities to either retrench the system or change it.

CREATIVE RESISTANCE

Conceiving the world as linked through a system of racial hierarchy shows that people's actions and inactions have tremendous effects across national boundaries, and that undoing racism requires acting in ways sensitive to this globality. The racial subjugation of native populations in Peru is only comprehensible through seeing the international dimensions of the system, of a rentier bourgeoisie dependent on repressing national populations on behalf of and empowered by global links.

As far as redressing this system, my analysis generally shows the need for creativity and overcoming all aspects of institutionalized segregation, including its international aspects. Obviously a very difficult task, some major keys include exploiting the multiple systemic irrationalities, and employing rentier windfalls to assert political regimes of full citizen participation guaranteeing fundamental rights from which to build meaningful lives, as has been demonstrated in a very few localities such as Kerala, India. As economists such as John Kenneth Galbraith have shown for almost fifty years that the means of production have been sufficiently advanced to eradicate world poverty, the solution is not economic but political and about distribution. And as this book has hopefully demonstrated, paternalism has no place, perhaps providing some redistributive relief but at the cost of shoring up the entire exploitative system. In other words, the industrial bourgeoisie succeeded long ago in their historical mission of revolutionizing the means of production; it remains to the rest of us to see the fruits of this serve humanity.

The historic record in Peru shows that the indigenous population and their allies have variously and creatively fought for inclusive political systems, a goal that has been regularly economically and sometimes even politically feasible. The strengths of the existing system, what has enabled it to endure for so long, and what has made it such a tenacious foe, are (1) the quick reliance on military reprisals, and (2) the intertwining ways that indirect rule makes discontent reinforce rather than undermine the system. So successful challenges must leverage their advances into other parts of the system or risk reproducing it.

The Evangelical revitalization of Huaytabamba proves instructive. This creatively derived form of organization, generally unthreatening to systemic sensibilities, successfully built a vibrant means for meaningful political participation at the village level such that, even within the confines of developmentalist exploitation, it improved the overall wellbeing of inhabitants. This movement came up short in two key ways. First, it never challenged the anti-politics and paternalism of developmentalism. The inclusive political infrastructure did not delve into helping define the parameters of the development machinery—it mostly focused on choosing which program to participate in. And while it challenged the exploitative character of paternalist project delivery, it did not marshal its political infrastructure to challenge the overall exploitative nature of the system.

This may have been beyond the capacity of a single village, requiring meaningful networks to similarly situated people. In this, the attempt to establish alternative connections to external organizations in the fight against privatization was a real opportunity. Had they been able to sufficiently redress these organizations' racism to make these links, they had the real possibility of launching the anti-privatization struggle into broader political achievements. And maybe better international connections could have worked to empower this attempt at anti-racist political self-determination. Finally, while the anything to anyone nature of Evangelicism may have undermined the capacity to network with brothers, the content of ethnic revitalization is much more broadly shared and potentially linkable—though always risking the exploitative strand of such ethnic relations.

NOTE

1. For a similar comparative methodology, see Burawoy (1982).

Bibliography

Adams, Douglas. 2004. *The Hitchhiker's Guide to the Galaxy*. New York: Harmony Books.

Albó, X. 1994. "Ethnic Violence: The Case of Bolivia." In K. Rupesinghe (ed.), *The Culture of Violence*. United Nations University Press.

Allen, Catherine. 1988. *The Hold Life Has: Coca and Cultural Identity in an Andean Community*. Washington, DC: Smithsonian Institute.

Annis, Sheldon. 1987. *God and Production in a Guatemalan Town*. Austin: University of Texas Press.

Ansell, A. 2006. "Casting a Blind Eye." *Critical Sociology* 32(2–3): 333–356.

Appelbaum, Nancy P., Anne S. Macpherson, and Karin Alejandra Rosemblatt. 2003. *Race and Nation in Modern Latin America*. Chapel Hill: University of North Carolina Press.

Baiocchi, Gianpaolo. 2001. "Participation, Activism, and Politics: The Porto Alegre Experiment and Deliberative Democratic Theory." *Politics & Society* 29(1): 43–72.

Bastian, Jean-Pierre. 1993. "The Metamorphosis of Latin American Protestant Groups: A Sociohistorical Perspective." *Latin American Research Review* 28: 33–62.

Bonilla, Heraclio. 1974. *Guano y Burguesía en el Perú*. Lima: IEP.

Bonilla-Silva, E. 1997. "Rethinking Racism." *American Sociological Review* 62(3): 465–480.

Bonilla-Silva, E. 2001. *White Supremacy and Racism in the Post-Civil Rights Era*. Lynne Rienner: Boulder.

Bourdieu, P. 1986. "The Forms of Capital." In J. Richardson (ed.), *Handbook of Theory and Research for the Sociology of Education*, 241–258. Greenwood Press: New York.

Bourdieu, P. 1998. "The Essence of Neoliberalism." U.st: Le Monde Diplomatique.

Bourricaud, F. 1968. "'Indian, Mestizo, and Cholo as Symbols of the Peruvian Stratification System." In J. Cotler, "La Mecánica de la Dominación Interna y del Cambio Social en el Perú." *Perú Problema*.

Brief, A., R. Buttram, J. Elliott, R. Reizenstein, and R. McCline. 1995. "Releasing the Beast: A Study of Compliance with Orders to Use Race as a Selection Criterion." *Journal of Social Issues* 51: 177–193.

Brusco, Elizabeth. 1993. "The Reformation of Machismo." In Virginia Garrard-Burnett and David Stoll (eds.), *Rethinking Protestantism in Latin America*, 143–158. Philadelphia: Temple University Press.

Burawoy, Michael. 1976. "The Functions and Reproduction of Migrant Labor: Comparative Material from Southern Africa and the United States." *American Journal of Sociology* 81(5): 1050–1087.

Burawoy, Michael. 1982. *Manufacturing Consent: Changes in the Labor Process under Monopoly Capitalism*. Chicago: University of Chicago Press.

Burdick, John. 1992. "Rethinking the Study of Social Movements." In Sonia E. Alvarez, Evelina Dagnino, and Arturo Escobar (eds.), *Cultures of Politics, Politics of Cultures*, 171–184. Boulder: Westview Press.

Burdick, John. 1993. "Struggling against the Devil: Pentecostalism and Social Movements in Urban Brazil." In Virginia Garrard-Burnett and David Stoll (eds.), *Rethinking Protestantism in Latin America*, 20–44. Philadelphia: Temple University Press.

Burdick, John. 1996. *Looking for God in Brazil: The Progressive Catholic Church in Urban Brazil's Religious Arena*. Berkeley: University of California Press.

Burga, Manuel, and Alberto Flores-Galindo. 1987. *Apageo y Crisis de la Republica Aristocrática*, 4th ed. Lima: Rikchay Peru.

Callirgos, J. C. 1993. *El racismo: La cuestión del otro (y de uno)*. Lima: DESCO Centro de Estudios y Promoción del Desarrollo.

Chang, Ha-Joon. 2008. *Bad Samaritans: The Myth of Free Trade and the Secret History of Capitalism*. New York, NY: Bloomsbury Press.

Chesnut, Andrew R. 1997. *Born Again in Brazil*. New Brunswick: Rutgers University Press.

Chesnut, Andrew R. 2003. *Competitive Spirits: Latin America's New Religious Economy*. Oxford [England]: Oxford University Press.

Coleman, Simon. 2000. *The Globalisation of Charismatic Christianity: Spreading the Gospel of Prosperity*. Cambridge: Cambridge University Press.

Collins, Jane. 1988. *Unseasonal Migrations*, Princeton: Princeton University Press.

Collins, P. 1996. *Black Feminist Thought*. Routledge: New York.

Colloredo-Mansfeld, R. J. 2009. *Fighting Like a Community: Andean Civil Society in an Era of Indian Uprisings*. Chicago: University of Chicago Press.

D'Epinay, Christian Lalive. 1967. *Haven of the Masses: A Study of the Pentecostal Movement in Chile*. London, Lutterworth Press.

De la Cadena, Marisol. 2000. *Indigenous Mestizos*. Durham: Duke University Press.

Degregori, C. 1995. "El Estudio del Otro." In J. Cotler (ed.), *Peru 1964–1994*, 303–32. IEP: Lima.

Del Pino, Ponciano. 1996. "Tiempos de guerra y de dioses." In Carlos Ivan Degregori (ed.), *Las Rodans Campesinas*, 117–188. Lima: IEP.

Dijkstra, Geske. 2005. "The PRSP Approach and the Illusion of Improved Aid Effectiveness: Lessons from Bolivia, Honduras and Nicaragua." *Development Policy Review* 23(4): 443–464.

Drinot, Paulo. 2006. "Nation-Building, Racism and Inequality: Institutional Development in Peru in Historical Perspective." In J. Crabtree (ed.), *Making Institutions Work in Peru: Democracy, Development and Inequality since 1980*. London: Institute for the Study of the Americas, University of London.

Drinot, Paulo. 2011. "The Meaning of Alan García: Sovereignty and Governmentality in Neoliberal Peru." *Journal of Latin American Cultural Studies* 20(2): 179–195.

Dyer, R. 1988. "White." *Screen* 29(44): 115–119.

Evans, Peter. 2004. "Development as Institutional Change: The Pitfalls of Monocropping and the Potentials of Deliberation." *Studies in Comparative International Development* 38(4): 30–52.

Flores Galindo, A. 1988. *Buscando un Inca*. Lima, Perú: Editorial Horizonte.

Foucault, Michel. 2000. *Power. Volume 3 of Essential Works of Foucault: 1954–1984*. New York: The New Press.

Freston, Paul. 1995. "Pentecostalism in Brazil: A Brief History." *Religion* 25(2): 119–133.

Freston, Paul. 2001. *Evangelicals and Politics in Asia, Africa, and Latin America*. Cambridge: Cambridge University Press.

Freston, Paul. 2008. *Evangelical Christianity and Democracy in Latin America*. Oxford: Oxford University Press.

Galeano, Eduardo. 1976. *Open Veins of Latin America: Five Centuries of the Pillage of a Continent*. New York: Monthly Review Press.

García, María Elena, and José Antonio Lucero. 2004. "Un País sin Indigenas?" In Nancy Grey Postero and Leon Zamasc (eds.), *The Struggle for Inidigenous Rights in Latin America*. Portland: Sussex Academic Press.

Garrard-Burnett, Virginia. 1993. "Conclusion: Is This Latin America's Reformation?" In Virginia Garrard-Burnett and David Stoll (eds.), *Rethinking Protestantism in Latin America*, 199–210. Philadelphia: Temple University Press.

Garrard-Burnett, Virginia. 2004. "'God was Already Here when Columbus Arrived': Inculturation Theology and the Mayan Movement in Guatemala." In Edward L. Cleary and Timothy J. Steigenga (eds.), *Resurgent Voices in Latin America: Indigenous*

Peoples, Political Mobilization, and Religious Change, 125–153. New Brunswick, NJ: Rutgers University Press.

Garrett, D. T. 2004. "'His Majesty's Most Loyal Vassals': The Indian Nobility and Tupac Amaru." *Hispanic American Historical Review* 84 (4): 575–617.

Gaskill, Newton J. 1997. "Rethinking Protestantism and Democratic Consolidation in Latin America." *Sociology of Religion* 58: 1.

Goldberg, D. 2002. *The Racial State*. Malden, MA: Blackwell Publishers.

Goldberg, D. 2009. *The Threat of Race*. Malden, MA: Wiley-Blackwell.

Gonzales de Olarte, E. 1998. *El Neoliberalismo a la Peruana*. IEP: Lima.

Gootenberg, Paul. 1993. *Imagining Development: Economic Ideas in Peru's "Fictitious Prosperity" of Guano, 1840–1880*. Berkeley: University of California Press.

Gose, P. 1994. "Embodied Violence." In D. Poole (ed.), *Unruly Order*, 165–198. Boulder: Westview.

Green, Linda. 1993. "Shifting Affiliations: Mayan Widows and *Evangélicos* in Guatemala." In Virginia Garrard-Burnett and David Stoll (eds.), *Rethinking Protestantism in Latin America*, 159–179. Philadelphia: Temple University Press.

Grieshaber, E. P. 1979. "Hacienda-Indian Community Relations and Indian Acculturation: An Historiographical Essay." *Latin American Research Review* 14(3): 107–128.

Guinier, Lani, and Gerald Torres. 2002. *The Miner's Canary: Enlisting Race, Resisting Power, Transforming Democracy*. Cambridge, MA: Harvard University Press.

Hale, C. 1997. "Cultural Politics of Identity in Latin America." *Annual Review Anthropology* 26: 567–590.

Hale, C. 2002. "Does Multiculturalism Menace?" *Journal of Latin American Studies* 34: 3.

Hale, C. 2004. "Rethinking Indigenous Politics in the Era of the 'Indio Permitido.'" *NACLA Report on the Americas* 38(2): 16–22.

Hale, C. 2006. *Más que un Indio*. Santa Fe: School of American Research.

Hale, C. 2008. *Engaging Contradictions: Theory, Politics, and Methods of Activist Scholarship*. Berkeley: University of California Press.

Hall, S. 1980. "Race Articulation and Societies Structured in Dominance." In *Sociological Theories: Race and Colonialism*, 305–345. Paris: UNESCO.

Harvey, David. 2003. *The New Imperialism*. Oxford: Oxford University Press.

Harvey, David. 2005. *A Brief History of Neoliberalism*. New York: Oxford University Press.

Heilman, Jaymie Patricia. 2010. *Before the Shining Path: Politics in Rural Ayacucho, 1895–1980*. Stanford, CA: Stanford University Press.

Holdaway, S. 1997. "Some Recent Approaches to the Study of Race in Criminological Research." *British Journal of Criminology* 37(3): 383–400.

Ireland, Rowan. 1999. "Popular Religions and the Building of Democracy in Latin America: Saving the Tocquevillian Parallel." *Journal of Interamerican Studies and World Affairs* 41(4): 111–146.

Isbell, Billie Jean. 1978. *To Defend Ourselves: Ecology and Ritual in an Andean Village*. Austin: University of Texas Press.

Isbister, J. 1997. *Promises not Kept: The Betrayal of Social Change in the Third World*. West Hartford, CT: Kumarian Press.

Kamsteeg, Frans H. 1998. *Prophetic Pentecostalism in Chile: A Case Study on Religion and Development Policy*. Lanham: Scarecrow Press.

Kay, Cristobal. 1981. "Achievements and Contradictions of the Peruvian Agrarian Reform." *Journal of Development Studies* 18: 6.

Klarén, P. 2000. *Peru: Society and Nationhood in the Andes*. New York: Oxford University Press.

Lagos, M. 1994. *Autonomy and Power: the Dynamics of Class and Culture in Rural Bolivia*. Philadelphia: University of Pennsylvania Press.

Li, Tania Murray. 2010. "To Make Live or Let Die? Rural Dispossession and the Protection of Surplus Populations." *Antipode* 41 (Supplement): 66–93.

Li, Tania Murray. 2011. "Centering Labor in the Land Grab Debate." *Journal of Peasant Studies* 38(2): 281–298.

Lim, Chaeyoon, and Robert D. Putnam. 2010. "Religion, Social Networks, and Life Satisfaction." *American Sociological Review* 75(6): 914–933.

Lipsitz, G. 1995. "The Possessive Investment in Whiteness." *American Quarterly* 47(3): 369–387.

Lucero, J. A. 2008. *Struggles of Voice: The Politics of Indigenous Representation in the Andes.* Pittsburgh, PA: University of Pittsburgh Press.

MacIsaac, D., and H. Patrinos. 1995. "Labor Market Discrimination against Indigenous People in Peru." *Journal of Development Studies* 32(2): 218–233.

Mallon, Florencia. 1983. *The Defense of Community in Peru's Central Highlands.* Princeton: Princeton University Press.

Mallon, Florencia. 1992. "Indian Communities, Political Cultures, and the State in Latin America, 1780–1990." *Journal of Latin American Studies* 24(Supplement): 35–53.

Mallon, Florencia. 1995. *Peasant and Nation.* Berkeley: University of California Press.

Mallon, Florencia. 1998. "Chronicle of a Path Foretold?" In Steve J. Stern (ed.), *Shining and Other Paths.* Durham: Duke University Press.

Mamdani, M. 1996. *Citizen and Subject.* Princeton: Princeton University Press.

Manrique, Nelson. 1999. *La piel y la pluma: Escritos sobre literatura, etnicidad y racismo.* San Isidro [Perú]: CIDIAG.

Manrique, N. 2000. "Modernity and Alternative Development in the Andes." In Schelling (ed.), *Through the Kaleidoscope: The Experience of Modernity in Latin America. Critical Studies in Latin American and Iberian Cultures.* New York: Verso.

Marcuse, Herbert. 1960. "Epilogue to the New German Edition of Karl Marx's *18th Brumaire of Louis Napoleon.*" *Radical America* III(4): 55–59.

Martin, David. 1990. *Tongues of Fire: The Explosion of Protestantism in Latin America.* Oxford: Basil Blackwell.

Marx, Karl. 1844. *Economic & Philosophic Manuscripts.* Marxist Internet Archive. https://www.marxists.org/archive/marx/works/1844/manuscripts/preface.htm.

Marx, Karl. 1848. *Manifesto of the Communist Party.* Marxist Internet Archive. https://www.marxists.org/archive/marx/works/1848/communist-manifesto/index.htm.

Marx, Karl. 1852. *The Eighteenth Brumaire of Lois Napoleon.* Marxist Internet Archive. https://www.marxists.org/archive/marx/works/1852/18th-brumaire/.

Marx, Karl. 1867. *Capital.* Marxist Internet Archive. https://www.marxists.org/archive/marx/works/1867-c1/.

Maxwell, David. 1998. "'Delivered from the Spirit of Poverty?' Pentecostalism, Prosperity and Modernity in Zimbabwe." *Journal of Religion in Africa* 28(3): 350–373.

Mayer, Enrique. 1985. "Production Zones." In Yoshio Masuda, Izumi Shimada, and Craig Morris (eds.), *Andean Ecology and Civilization,* 45–84. Tokyo: University of Tokyo Press.

Meyer, Birgit. 1995. "'Delivered from the Powers of Darkness': Confessions of Satanic Riches in Christian Ghana." *Africa* 65(2): 236–255.

Meyer, Birgit. 1999. *Translating the Devil.* Trenton, NJ: Africa World Press.

Mignolo, Walter. 2000. *Local Histories/Global Designs: Coloniality, Subaltern Knowledges, and Border Thinking.* Princeton, NJ: Princeton University Press.

Mills, Charles. 1998. *Blackness Visible.* Ithaca: Cornell.

Mills, Charles. 2000. "Global White Supremacy." In Paula S. Rothenberg (ed.), *White Privilege: Essential Readings on the Other Side of Racism.* New York: Worth Publishers.

Ministerio de Agricultura. 2004. *Portal Agrario: Titulación de Tierras.* http://www.portalagrario.gob.pe/tc_impactos.shtml, 4/2/04.

Moreno, Pedro. 1999. "Evangelical Churches." In Paul E. Sigmund (ed.), *Religious Freedom and Evangelization in Latin America,* 49–69. Maryknoll, NY: Orbis.

Morner, M. 1966. *Race Mixture in the History of Latin America.* Boston: Little Brown.

Morrison, Kevin M., and Matthew M. Singer. 2007. "Inequality and Deliberative Development: Revisiting Bolivia's Experience with the PRSP." *Development Policy Review* 25(6): 721–740.

Muratorio, Blanca. 1982. *Etnicidad, Evangelización y Protesta en el Ecuador.* Quito: Centro de Investigaciones y Estudios Socio-Económicos.

Neckerman, K., and J. Kirschenman. 1991. "'We'd Love to Hire Them But.'" *Social Problems* 38(4): 433–447.

Nugent, Guillermo. 2005. "La Desigualdad es una bandera de papel." *Peru Hoy*, 205–227. Lima: desco.

Nylen, William R. 2003. *Participatory Democracy versus Elitist Democracy: Lessons from Brazil*. New York: Palgrave Macmillan.

Omi, M., and H. Winant. 1994. *Racial Formation in the United States*, 2nd ed. Routledge: New York.

Ong, A. 2006. *Neoliberalism as Exception: Mutations in Citizenship and Sovereignty*. Durham, NC: Duke University Press.

Pager, D., and L. Quillian. 2005. "Walking the Talk? What Employers Say Versus What They Do." *American Sociological Review* 70: 355–380.

Petras, J., and M. Morley. 1992. *Latin America in the Time of Cholera*. Routledge: New York.

Piketty, Thomas, and Arthur Goldhammer. 2013. *Capital in the Twenty-First Century*. Cambridge, MA: The Belknap Press of Harvard University Press.

Poole, D. 1994. *Unruly Order: Violence, Power, and Cultural Identity in the High Provinces of Southern Peru*. Boulder: Westview Press.

Poole, D. 2004. "Between Threat and Guarantee: Justice and Community in the Margins of the Peruvian State," in V. Das and D. Poole, *Anthropology in the Margins of the State*. School of American Research Advanced Seminar Series. Santa Fe, NM: School of American Research Press.

Portocarrero, G. 1993. "Castigo sin Culpa, Culpa sin Castigo." *Racismo y Mestisaje*, 33–96. Lima: SUR.

Portocarrero, G. 2007. *Racismo y mestizaje y otros ensayos*. Lima: Fondo Ed. del Congreso del Perú.

Postero, N. 2007. *Now We Are Citizens*. Stanford: Stanford University Press.

PTRT Programa de Titulación y Regístro de Tierras. 2001. *Perfil II: Peru*. Santiago, Chile: FAO.

Quijano, A. 2000. "Coloniality of Power and Eurocentrism in Latin America." *International Sociology* 15: 215–232.

Renique, José Luis. 1994. "Political Violence, the State, and the Peasant Struggle for Land (Puno)." In Poole (ed.), *Unruly Order*. Boulder: Westview Press.

Robbins, Joel. 2004. "The Globalization of Pentecostal and Charismatic Christianity." *Annual Review of Anthropology* 33: 117–143.

Roberts, Keith A. 1995. *Religion in Sociological Perspective*. Boston: Wadsworth.

Robinson, W. I. 2004. *A Theory of Global Capitalism*. Baltimore: Johns Hopkins University Press.

Robinson, W. I. 2013. "Global Capitalism and its Anti-'Human Face': Organic Intellectuals and Interpretations of the Crisis." *Globalizations* 10(5): 659–671.

Roniger, L., and A. Güneş-Ayata. 1994. *Democracy, Clientelism, and Civil Society*. L. Rienner: Boulder.

Rotta Castilla, S., and L. Narvarte Olivares. 2006. "Peru." *Transparency International Global Corruption Report 2006*.

Sanchez, Rafael. 2008. "Seized by the Spirit: The Mystical Foundation of Squatting among Pentecostals in Caracas (Venezuela) Today." *Public Culture: Bulletin of the Project for Transnational Cultural Studies* 20(2): 267–306.

Sassen, Saskia. 2010. "A Savage Sorting of Winners and Losers: Contemporary Versions of Primitive Accumulation." *Globalizations* 7(1–2): 23–50.

Sassen, Saskia. 2012. "Expanding the Terrain for Global Capital." In Manuel B. Aalbers (ed.), *Subprime Cities: The Political Economy of Mortgage Markets*, First Edition, 74–96.

Sassen, Saskia. 2014. *Expulsions: Brutality and Complexity in the Global Economy*. Cambridge, MA: The Belknap Press of Harvard University Press.

Scarritt, Arthur. 2010. "Essentializing Authoritarianism: Implementing Neoliberalism in Highland Peru." *The Applied Anthropologist* 30(1–2): 27–33.

Scarritt, Arthur. 2011. "Broker Fixed: the Racialized Social Structure and the Subjuga-
  tion of Indigenous Populations in the Andes." *Critical Sociology*, 37(2): 153–177.
Scarritt, Arthur. 2012. "State of Discord: the Historic Reproduction of Racism in High-
  land Peru." *Postcolonial Studies* 15(1): 23–44.
Scarritt, Arthur. 2013. "First the Revolutionary Culture: Innovations in Empowered
  Citizenship from Evangelical Highland Peru." *Latin American Perspectives*, 40(4):
  101–120.
Schatz, E. 2009. *Political Ethnography: What Immersion Contributes to the Study of Power*.
  Chicago: The University of Chicago Press.
Schwalbe, M., S. Godwin, D. Holden, D. Schrock, S. Thompson, and M. Wolkomir.
  January 1, 2000. "Generic Processes in the Reproduction of Inequality: An Interac-
  tionist Analysis." *Social Forces* 79(2): 419–452.
Smilde, David. 2003. "Evangelicals and Politics in Latin America: Moving Beyond
  Monolithic Portraits." *History of Religions* 42(3): 243–248.
Smith, Christian, and Liesl Ann Hass. 1997. "Revolutionary Evangelicals in Nicaragua:
  Political Opportunity, Class Interests, and Religious Identity." *Journal for the Scien-
  tific Study of Religion* 36(3): 440–454.
Spalding, K. 1970. "Social Climbers: Changing Patterns of Mobility among the Indians
  of Colonial Peru." *Hispanic American Historical Review* 50(4): 645–664.
Spalding, K. 1973. "Kurakas and Commerce: A Chapter in the Evolution of Andean
  Society." *Hispanic American Historical Review* 53(4): 581–599.
Spalding, K. 1975. "Hacienda-Village Relations in Andean Society to 1830." *Latin
  American Perspectives* 2(1): 107–121.
Steigenga, Timothy J. 2001. *The Politics of the Spirit: The Political Implications of Pentecos-
  talized Religion in Costa Rica and Guatemala*. Lanham, MD: Lexington Books.
Steigenga, Timothy J., and Kenneth Coleman. 1995. "Protestant Political Orientations
  and the Structure of Political Opportunity: Chile, 1972–1991." *Polity* 27(3): 465–482.
Stern, S. J. 1992. *Peru's Indian Peoples and the Challenge of Spanish Conquest: Huamanga to
  1640*, 2nd ed. Madison, WI: University of Wisconsin Press.
Stokes, S. C. 1995. *Cultures in Conflict: Social Movements and the State in Peru*. Berkeley:
  University of California Press.
Stoll, David. 1990. *Is Latin America Turning Protestant?* Berkeley: University of Califor-
  nia Press.
Stoll, David. 1993. *Between Two Armies in the Ixil Town of Guatemala*. New York: Colum-
  bia University Press.
Stoll, David. 2013. *El Norte or Bust: How Migration Fever and Microcredit Produced a
  Financial Crash in a Latin American Town*. Lanham, MD: Rowman & Littlefield Pub-
  lishing.
Thiele, Rainer. 1991. *Peruvian Agriculture: Recent History, Present Performance and the
  Effects of Agricultural and General Economic Policies*. Kiel: Kiel Institute of World
  Economics.
Thorp, Rosemary, and Geoffrey Bertram. 1978. *Peru 1890–1977: Growth and Policy in an
  Open Economy*. New York: Columbia University Press.
Thurner, M. 1995. "'Republicanos' and 'la Comunidad de Peruanos': Unimagined Po-
  litical Communities in Postcolonial Andean Peru." *Journal of Latin American Studies*
  27(2): 291.
Thurner, M. 1997. "Atusparia and Cáceres." *Hispanic American Historical Review* 77(3):
  409–421.
Tilly, C. 1998. *Durable Inequality*. Berkeley: University of California Press.
Transparency International. 2006. *Global Corruption Report 2006*. Transparency Interna-
  tional.
Van den Berghe, P., and G. Primov. 1977. *Inequality in the Peruvian Andes*. Columbia:
  University of Missouri Press.
Vargas Llosa, M. 1990. "Questions of Conquest." *Harper's Magazine* (December): 45–53.
Vasconcelos, J. 1979 [1925]. *La Raza Cósmica*. Los Angeles: California State University.
Wade, P. 1997. *Race and Ethnicity in Latin America*. Chicago: Pluto Press.

Walker, C. 1999. *Smoldering Ashes: Cuzco and the Creation of Republican Peru, 1780–1840*. Durham, NC: Duke University Press.

Wampler, Brian. 2004. "Expanding Accountability through Participatory Institutions: Mayors, Citizens, and Budgeting in Three Brazilian Municipalities." *Latin American Politics & Society* 46(2): 73–99.

Wampler, Brian. 2007. *Participatory Budgeting in Brazil: Contestation, Cooperation, and Accountability*. University Park, PA: Pennsylvania State University Press.

Warren, K., and J. Jackson. 2003. *Indigenous Movements, Self-Representation, and the State in Latin America*. Austin: University of Texas Press.

Weber, M. 1968 [1922]. *Economy and Society*. New York: Bedminster Press.

Weismantel, M. 1988. *Food, Gender, and Poverty in the Ecuadorian Andes*. Philadelphia: University of Pennsylvania Press.

Weismantel, M., and S. Eisenman. 1998. "Race in the Andes: Global Movements and Popular Ontologies." *Bulletin of Latin American Research* 17(2): 121–142.

Winant, H. 2001. *The World is a Ghetto*. New York: Basic Books.

Wolf, Eric R. 1956. "Aspects of Group Relations in a Complex Society: Mexico." *American Anthropologist* 58: 6.

Wolf, E. 1982. *Europe and the People without History*. Berkeley: University of California Press.

Wolf, Eric R., and Edward C. Hansen. 1972. *The Human Condition in Latin America*. New York: Oxford University Press.

World Bank. 2005. "Indigenous Peoples, Poverty and Human Development in Latin America: 1994–2004." Washington, DC: World Bank.

Yashar, Deborah J. 2005. *Contesting Citizenship in Latin America*. New York: Cambridge University Press.

Yezer, Caroline. 2008. "Who Wants to Know? Rumors, Suspicions, and Opposition to Truth-telling in Ayacucho." *Latin American and Caribbean Ethnic Studies* 3(3): 271–289.

Zimmerer, Karl. 1996. *Changing Fortunes*. Berkeley: University of California Press.

Žižek, Slavoj. 2012. *The Year of Dreaming Dangerously*. London: Verso.

Index

About the Author

Arthur Scarritt is associate professor in the Department of Sociology at Boise State University. He is interested in how people navigate the multiple differences in their lives, especially race, class, and gender. In particular, he looks at the innovative ways people both reproduce and challenge inequalities. After conducting years of fieldwork in the Andes, Scarritt is focusing more attention on inequalities in higher education, particularly the way that the "business model" of neoliberal privatization creates novel ways to make itself seemingly inevitable and even invaluable. He has three wonderful children and an incredible wife.